Hajimete no Ninongo

はじめての　にほんご

<Level 1>
Japanese for Beginners

DARUMA DOLL: だるま さん　DARUMA SAN

Daruma san is one of Japan's folk toys. The arms or legs are not shown because it is wrapped by a blanket. The name comes from a Buddist priest who was enlighted after sitting for many years wrapped with a red blanket under severe conditions. The bottom of the doll is weighted so that if it is knocked over, it will right itself. People who want to achieve a goal paint one eye of darma. When they meet their goal, they color in the other eye.

Make your own *Daruma san*
<u>Materials</u>: paper strips, oval balloons, wheat paste, paint, paint brushes

<u>Steps</u>
1. Blow up oval ballon.
2. Dunk paper strips in wheat past. Put wet strips on blown up balloon.
3. Let dry.
3. Put extra layers of paper on the bottom. By doing that, it makes the figure heavy on the bottom, so that if it tips over, it will right itself.
4. Paint the robe and the face, but not the eyes.

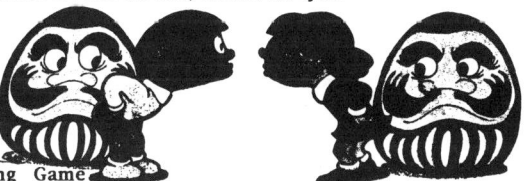

Chanting Game
Sit in a circle, with arms and legs crossed. Sway from side to side and chant:
darumasan, darumasan, niramekko shimasho. (Let's stare each other.)
warattara dame yo. (Don't laugh.) *untoko dokkoisho*
Make funniest face and try other laugh. Who has a strong will?

Title: JAPANESE FOR BEGINNERS, LEVEL 1
Hajimete no Nihongo はじめての　にほんご　1

Author: Noyuri Soderland
Published by Logos School of Languages Publishing
Fourth edition, 2000; Copyright 1982, 1985, 1993, 2000
ISBN: 0-9634141-1-9

Textbook: A Japanese textbook as a foreign language
Audience level: beginners
Age: junior & senior high school and adult group

Content: Six lessons, Appendix, Glossary
Written in Romanized Japanese and kana,
with translation
With illustrations
Accompanied by two 60 minutes cassette tapes

168 pages, 4 - 1/4 x 5.5 inches, perfect bound
Manufactured in USA

Address: Logos School of Languages Publishing
9208 Lovgreen Road, Bainbridge Island, Washington 98110 USA
Telephone: (206) 780-9231   Fax: (206) 842-6683
E-mail: Soderlan@bainbridge.net

About the writer

Education:

Japanese teaching certificate at University of Massachusetts
Linguistics B.A. at University of Washington
Graduated Himeji Junior College (Japan)

Taught Japanese at:

Edmonds School District in WA [high schools, home school (K-12)]
Springfield S.D. in MA (K - 8)
Kent S.D. In WA (high school)
Northwest schools in WA (high school)
University of Washington (College level)
The Language School in WA
 Logos School of Languages in WA

Published:
Japanese Through Songs
Japanese for Beginners, Level 1, 2, 3
Workbook 1: Katsudo no Tomo

Preface

The series, Hajimete no Nihongo, is written to make learning Japanese easy, meaningful and fun. Over the years, in teaching high school and college students, children, travelers, and people having business contacts with Japan, I have developed a lively, playful approach. This book reflects that light mood while systematically teaching the basic grammar of Japanese.

This book concentrates on the most useful sentence patterns and expressions. The goal is effective, practical communication. You will be pleased to find that the basic grammar of Japanese is not complicated when presented in an orderly way.

A good attitude as a student is to accept Japanese as a language different from your own. Listen to the sounds with a relaxed mind. Don't be in a hurry to get everything right. Imitate the sounds playfully as a baby does. Learn to think in Japanese without asking why things are said a certain way. Let Japanese become a part of you.

In the classroom activities, you will have a chance to respond physically or with short answers to the teacher. By the time you need to say more complicated expressions, you will have heard them from the teacher several times, naturally. This is the way a small child learns, with listening comprehension developing faster than speaking.

It's important to listen to the language tapes at least 10 minutes every day. Listen until you can easily understand the natural speed of Japanese. After a while it will no longer sound foreign to you. Don't try too hard to repeat the words from the tape until you can do so easily.

To the Teacher:

You are encouraged to improvise within the main grammatical theme of each lesson. Add or eliminate vocabulary to fit the students' situations. It's important for the students to actually act out the exercises. Students who can do so easily can take the teacher's role in dialogs and exercises.

The tapes are to be used at home and not in the classroom. You do not need to emphasize writing of hiragana and katakana. Learning to recognize the characters is enough at this point, for those students who are interested.

Table of Contents

LET'S PRACTICE SOME MORE at the end of each lesson includes:
Vocabulary builders:
Make cards, Listen and stand up,
Listen and line up, Spread cards on the table,
Shoots and ladders game, Around the world game
Quick draw + Full house bingo
PICTIONARY, FULL HOUSE BINGO, STORY TELLING
Match English - Japanese, Matching: B's response to A
Changing postive and negative, Fill in ( ), Choose one,
Make conjugation list
Guessing game, About myself, Inerview
Two way bingo, Constructing a sentence
A letter to your pen pal
Evaluation: Listening comprehension
Speaking 1, Speaking 2
Reading and writing

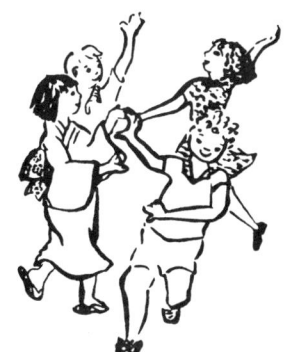

Introductory Lesson: **Greetings, Classroom**

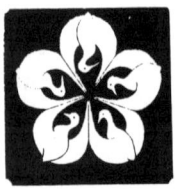

1. If you went to Japan right now,...
The text is read from # 16 in this lesson.

you would understand very little of what you heard. It does no good to get frustrated. The best approach is to just listen with a relaxed mind and guess, and guess. Quite often you will guess incorrectly. But when you begin to find a few words that you know, or that you have heard before, you have started on the road to a full understanding of Japanese. Please <u>listen to the language tapes often</u>, but without trying hard. Let the sounds and rhythms of Japanese enter your mind naturally.

2. The teacher takes roll

Teacher: Smith, Bob さん	
Smith, Bob san.	Bob Smith.
Bob Smith: はい	
Hai.	Yes.

Note that the family name is first. -<u>san</u> is added at end, after given name. Use after another person's name, but never after your own name.

3. You want to find out your new classmates' names

Bob: どなたですか。	
Donata desu ka.	Who are you?
Ann: Kelly Ann です。	
Kelly Ann desu.	I am Ann Kelly.
どうぞ　よろしく。	
Dōzo yoroshiku.	Glad to meet you. / Please remember me.

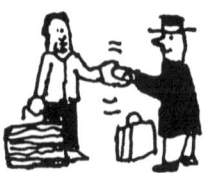

Ask each other's name

あなたの　なまえは　なんですか。
Anata no namae wa nan desu ka.　　　What is your name?

At the end of a sentence, 。 is placed like a period.
A particle は　is pronounced <u>wa</u> , not <u>ha.</u>

4. Ask about each other's health

Bob: Ann　さん、おげんきですか。
　　　Ann san, ogenki desu ka.　　　How are you, Ann?

Ann: げんきです。
　　　Genki desu.　　　　　I'm fine.

The honorific <u>o</u>- is placed before some words for politeness:
ogenki: for someone else's health　/　genki: for one's own health
Examples: ocha, osake, okashi, osushi, otanjobi, otomodachi, ohana

5. Greet each other at various times of day

a. おはよう　ございます。
　　Ohayō gozaimasu.　　　　Good morning.

b. こんにちは。
　　Kon-nichiwa.　　　　Hello. (daytime)

c. こんばんは。
　　Konbanwa.　　　　Hello. (after dark)

d. おやすみなさい。
　　Oyasumi nasai.　　　Good night. (lit. rest well)

6. Say goodbye when leaving the classroom

Ann: さようなら。
    Sayōnara.   Goodbye.

Bob: さようなら。
    Sayōnara.   Goodbye.

    また　あした。
    Mata ashita.   See you tomorrow.

    また　らいしゅう。
    Mata raishū.   See you next week.

    また　おあいしましょう。
    Mata oai shimashō.   See you again.

7. You are staying with a Japanese family
This is what you say when leaving the house for a while.

Ann: いって　まいります。
    Itte mairimasu.   I'm leaving now.

Mrs. Mori: いって　らっしゃい。
    Itte rasshai.   Come back soon.

These are not literal translations. English does not have an exact equivalent.

8. You say this when you come back home

Ann: ただいま。
    Tadaima.   I just got back.

Mrs. Mori: おかえり　なさい。
    Okaeri nasai.   Welcome home.

9. Act this out in class

A: おはよう　ございます。	Ohayō gozaimasu.
B: おはよう　ございます。	Ohayō gozaimasu.
A: いって　まいります。	Itte mairimasu.
B: いって　らっしゃい。	Itte rasshai.
A: ただいま。	Tadaima.
B: おかえりなさい。	Okaeri nasai.

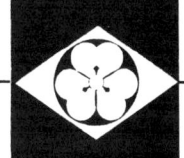

10. You are visiting a Japanese household
This is the greeting when entering the house.

Bob:	ごめんください。	
	Gomen kudasai.	Excuse me (for intruding)
Mrs. Mori:	いらっしゃいませ。	
	Irasshai mase.	Welcome.

11. After you have taken off your shoes at the entrance
and stepped up into the house, Mrs. Mori will lead you to the room for entertaining guests.

Mrs. Mori:	どうぞ　こちらへ。	
	Dōzo kochira e.	Please come this way.
Bob:	ありがとう　ございます。	
	Arigatō gozaimasu.	Thank you very much.

12. Mrs. Mori offers you some tea and cakes

Mrs. Mori:	おちゃは　いかがですか。	
	Ocha wa ikaga desu ka.	How about some tea?
Bob:	おねがい　します。	
	Onegai shimasu.	May I please?
Mrs. Mori:	どうぞ。	
	Dōzo.	Please (take some).
Bob:	すみません。	
	Sumimasen.	I'm sorry (to trouble you)
Mrs.Mori:	いいえ。	Iie. No (not at all).

13. You begin to eat

Bob: いただきます。
    Itadakimasu.   (I gratefully receive)
    ごちそうさま。
    Gochiso sama.   It was wonderful food.
Mrs. Mori: もう　いっぱい　いかがですか。
    Mō ippai ikaga desu ka.   How about another cup?
Bob: もう　けっこうです。
    Mō kekkō desu.   I've had enough./No, thank you.

14. The following was at the beginning of the language tape

as a listening comprehension exercise. How much can you recognize?

A: おはようございます。   Ohayō gozaimasu.
B: おはようございます。   Ohayō gozaimasu.

A: いってまいります。   Itte mairimasu.
B: いってらっしゃい。   Itte rasshai.
A: ごめんください。   Gomen kudasai.
C: いらっしゃいませ。   Irasshai mase.
   どなたですか。   Donata desu ka.
A: Smith Bob　です。   Smith Bob desu.
C: どうぞ　こちらへ。   Dōzo kochira e.
A: ありがとうございます。 Arigatō gozaimasu.

C: おちゃは　いかがですか。   Ocha wa ikaga desu ka.
A: おねがいします。   Onegai shimasu.
C: どうぞ。   Dōzo.
A: すみません。   Sumimasen.
C: いいえ。   Iie.
A: いただきます。ごちそうさま。 Itadakimasu. Gochisōsama.
C: もういっぱい　いかがですか。 Mō ippai ikaga desu ka.
A: もう　けっこうです。   Mō kekkō desu. Sayonara.
C: さようなら。また　おあいしましょう。
                    Sayōnara. Mata oai shimashō.

15. Classroom communication

a. わかりますか。
   Wakarimasu ka.   Do you understand?
b. わかりません。
   Wakarimasen.   I don't understand.
c. わかりました。
   Wakarimashita.   I have understood.

d. ほんを　おねがい　します。
   Hon o onegai shimasu.   May I have the book?
e. ゆっくり　おねがい　します。
   Yukkuri onegai shimasu.   Slowly, please.
f. もう　いちど　おねがい　します。
   Mō ichido onegai shimasu.   Once more, please.
g. ほんを　ください。
   Hon o kudasai.   Please give me the book.

h. ほんを　あけて　ください。
   Hon o akete kudasai.   Please open the book.
i. よんで　ください。
   Yonde kudasai.   Please read.
j. きいて　ください。
   Kiite kudasai.   Please listen.
k. かいて　ください。
   Kaite kudasai.   Please write.
l. こたえて　ください。
   Kotaete kudasai.   Please answer.
m. まって　ください。
   Matte kudasai.   Please wait.
n. いっしょに　いって　ください。
   Issho ni itte kudasai.   Please say it together.

o. いいですか。
   Ii desu ka.   Is it all right/good?
p. いいです。
   Ii desu.   It's fine/good.

16. Act this out in class.

Your teacher is having trouble understanding your foreign name:

T: すみません。　　　　　　　　　　Sumimasen.
　どなたですか。　　　　　　　　　Donata desu ka.
S: Smith Bob　です。　　　　　　　Smith Bob desu.
T: わかりません。　　　　　　　　　Wakarimasen.
　もういちど　いって　ください。　Mō ichido itte kudasai.
S: Smith Bobです。　　　　　　　　Smith Bob desu.
T: ゆっくり　いって　ください。　　Yukkuri itte kudasai.
S: Smith Bobです。　　　　　　　　Smith Bob desu.
T: かいて　ください。　　　　　　　Kaite kudasai.
　(Bob does so)
T: よんで　ください。　　　　　　　Yonde kudasai.
S: Bob Smith.
T: わかりました。　　　　　　　　　Wakarimashita.
　ありがとう　ございました。　　　Arigatō gozaimashita.
S: いいえ。　　　　　　　　　　　　Iie.

T: Bob　さん。きいてください。　　Bob san, kiite kudasai.
　こたえてください。　　　　　　　Kotaete kudasai.
　いいですか。　　　　　　　　　　Ii desu ka.
S: はい、いいです。　　　　　　　　Hai. Ii desu.

T: おちゃは　いかがですか。　　　　Ocha wa ikaga desu ka.
S: おねがい　します。　　　　　　　Onegai shimasu.
T: どうぞ。　　　　　　　　　　　　Dōzo.
S: ありがとう　ございます。　　　　Arigatō gozaimasu.
　いただきます。　　　　　　　　　Itadakimasu.
　ごちそうさま。　　　　　　　　　Gochisō sama.

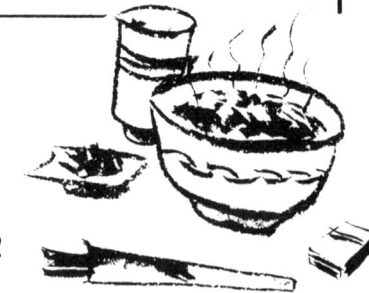

Page 12

LET'S PRACTICE SOME MORE
もっと　れんしゅう　しましょう。

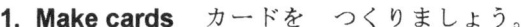

Vocabulary builders

1. Make cards　カードを　つくりましょう。
Make English-Japanese two-sided cards. Play card games in pairs, in a small group, or as a whole class. If the game requires two sets of cards, use the cards made by two students. Volunteers are wanted as game leaders.

2. Listen and stand up　きいて　たちましょう
Distribute a set of cards to a small group. Listen to the leader of the class. When you hear the word you have, stand up and show it. Who is the quickest?

3. Listen and line up　きいて　ならびましょう
Distribute a set of cards to a small group. Listen to the leader of the class, who will say five words; put down the corresponding cards in the same order. Which group lines up their cards in the correct order and the quickest?

4. Spread cards on the table　テーブルに　ひろげて
Spread a set of cards with English side facing up. Put your marker on a card and say it in Japanese. If it is the correct Japanese, it's yours; if it is not correct, leave it there. Go to the next player.

5. Shoots and ladders game　はしご　すごろく
Stack a set of cards with English side facing up.   Draw a card and say it in Japanese.

6. Around the world game せかい　いっしゅう　りょこう
Student A stands next to the seat of student B. An English side of one of the flash cards is shown to them. Both try to say it in Japanese. The first one who says it correctly is the winner. The loser sits in B's seat, and the winner moves on to challenge the student in the next seat. Continue as long as you like and see who has moved farthest from his original seat.

Quick draw + Full house bingo

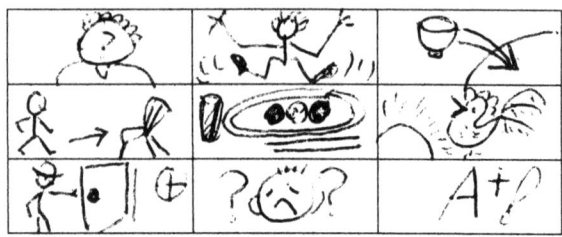

Activity A: PICTIONARY
Listen to one of the nine expressions, then draw to express the sentence in one of a 3x3 bingo grid. All nine pictures should be placed in random order.

Activity B: FULL HOUSE BINGO
Listen to one of the expressions and mark on the picture.
The winner says all the three expressions in a row.

Activity C: STORY TELLING: Tell a story using the pictures.

Expressions
1. Genki desu.
2. Ohayō gozaimasu.
3. Donata desu ka.
4. Dōzo kochira e.
5. Itadakimasu.
6. Wakarimasen.
7. Ii desu.
8. Gomen kudasai.
9. Ocha o onegai shimasu.

Match English - Japanese

a. Good evening   どなたですか。
b. I'm fine.   おげんきですか。
c. See you tomorrow.   こんにちは。
d. Glad to meet you.   こんばんは。
e. How are you?   また　あした。
f. Goodbye.   げんきです。
g. Who are you?   さようなら。
h. Hello. (daytime)   どうぞ　よろしく。
i. Good morning.   おはよう。

Match English - Japanese

a. Welcome home.   おちゃは　いかがですか。
b. Please come this way.   おねがい　します。
c. Thank you very much.   もう　けっこうです。
d. I'm leaving now.   おかえり　なさい。
e. I just got back.   すみません。
f. I've had enough.   ただいま。
g. How about some tea?   どうぞ　こちらへ。
h. I'm sorry.   いって　まいります。
i. May I please?   ありがとう　ございます。

Matching: B's response to A

A	B
a. Itte mairimasu.	Onegai shimasu.
b. Tadaima.	Mō kekkō desu.
c. Gomen kudasai.	Itte rasshai.
d. Dōzo kochira e.	Kelly Ann desu.
e. Ocha wa ikaga desu ka.	Okaeri nasai.
f. Mō ippai ikaga desu ka.	Irasshai mase.
g. Donata desu ka.	Arigatō gozaimasu.
h. Sayōnara.	Oyasumi nasai.
i. Oyasumi nasai.	Mata raishū.

A letter to your pen pal
Write a letter to your pen pal in Japanese and English.
Tell about yourself. Ask about your pen pal.
Example:

もり　みちよさん、
こんにちは。おげんきですか。
My name is Ann Kelly. どうぞ　よろしく。
I am a 17 year-old girl. How old are you? I am studying Japanese
at Central High School. What is the name of your school? I like
music and sports. What do you like? My birthday is December
12th. When is your birthday?
さようなら。おやすみなさい。　アン　ケリー

〒
POST

Evaluation: Listening comprehension

Listen to the Japanese expression. Which is the English equivalent?

1.
a. Good morning.
b. Good afternoon.
c. Good evening.
d. Good night.

2.
a. Goodbye.
b. How are you?
c. Thank you.
d. Please.

3.
a. Who are you?
b. Thank you very much.
c. I am fine.
d. Welcome (to my home).

4.
a. I'm leaving now.
b. Come back soon.
c. I just got back.
d. Welcome home.

5.
a. Excuse me (for intruding).
b. How about some tea?
c. May I have some tea?
d. How about another cup?

6.
a. See you tomorrow.
b. See you next week.
c. See you again.
d. Please come this way.

7.
a. Slowly, please.
b. Once more, please.
c. Please say it.
d. Please answer.

8.
a. I've had enough.
b. (said before eating)
c. (said after eating)
d. I'm sorry. Excuse me.

9.
a. Is it all right?
b. I don't understand.
c. I've got it.
d. Do you understand?

10.
a. Please read.
b. Please listen.
c. Please write.
d. Please wait.

Evaluation: Speaking 1

Say all the English expressions above in Japanese.

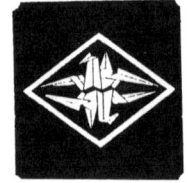

Evaluation: Speaking 2
1. Write a poster with 10 Japanese expressions you have learned. Illustrate the expressions.
2. Presentation: Talk in Japanese for one minute using your poster.

Conversation (example)

A: Ohayō gozaimasu.
B: Ohayō gozaimasu.
A: Ogenki desu ka.
B: Genki desu. Arigatō.
A: Itadakimasu. Gochisō sama.
B: Hon o mite kudasai.
A: Wakarimasen.
B: Hon o onegai shimasu.
A: Itte mairimasu.
B: Itte rasshai.

Interview (example)

1. Donata desu ka. - Ann desu.
2. Ogenki desu ka. - Genki desu. Arigatō gozaimasu.
3. Ocha wa ikaga desu ka. - Onegai shimasu.
4. Mō ippai ikaga desu ka. - Mō kekko desu.
5. Hon wa ikaga desu ka. - Hai, hon o kudasai.
6. Hon o yonde kudasai. - (Read)
7. Wakarimasu ka. - Hai, wakarimasu.
8. Mō ichido itte kudasai. - Hai, wakarimasu.
9. Arigatō. Sayōnara. - Sayōnara. Mata oai shimashō.
10. Mata ashita. - Mata ashita.

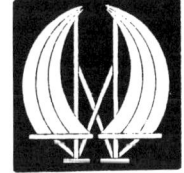

Scoring guide: date   name

a. Vocabulary: variety, new words	0	1	2	3	4
b. Sentence: variety, new structures	0	1	2	3	4
c. Attitude: gesture, eye contact	0	1	2	3	4
d. Voice: clear and natural	0	1	2	3	4
e. Memorized?	0	1	2	3	4

Your total points   / 20

Evaluation: Reading and writing

1. Who are you?
   （　　　）ですか。
2. I'm fine.
   （　　　）です。
3. See you tomorrow.
   また（　　　）。
4. Come back soon.
   （　　　）なさい。
5. Excuse me (for intruding)
   ごめん（　　　）。
6. Please come this way.
   どうぞ（　　　）。
7. How about some tea?
   おちゃは（　　　）ですか。
8. Slowly please.
   （　　　）おねがい　します。
9. Is it all right?
   （　　　）ですか。
10. Please listen.
   きいて（　　　）。

さくら さくら

の やまも さとも

みわたす かぎり

かすみか くもか

あさひに におう

さくら さくら　はなざかり

sakura sakura	Cherry blossoms, cherry blossoms
no yama mo sato mo	Field, mountains and villages, too
miwatasu kagiri	As far as we can see
kasumi ka kumo ka	Is it mist? or clouds?
asahi ni niou	Fragrance in the morning sun
sakura sakura	Cherry blossoms, cherry blossoms
hana zakari	in full bloom

1. Cherry blossom front line, *sakura zensen*
Sakura is the Japanese national flower. In spring, newspapers report, just like a weather report, where and how many *sakura* are in bloom. Japanese islands stretch from south to north, with *sakura* starting to open in the south and day by day moving to the north.

2. Flower viewing *Hanami*
Go and sit under a *sakura* tree with your family and friends. Make *onigiri*, rice balls and take them to *hanami*. Play games and sports. Draw pictures and make poems and *haiku*. Sing and dance, eat and drink, talk and laugh.

3. Make *origami* flowers.
Make flowers of various colors, sizes and petal shapes. They can be good gifts for many occasions.

4. Conversation
A: なんの はなですか。
　 nan no hana desu ka.　What flower is it?
B: (さくら)の はなです。
　 (sakura) no hana desu.　It is a cherry flower.

5. Useful expression
(さくら)は はなざかり です。
(sakura)wa hana zakari desu.　Cherry blossoms are in full bloom.

さくら sakura cherrry	の no field	やま yama mountain	さと sato village	かすみ kasumi mist	くも kumo cloud	あさひ asahi morning sun	におう niou smell	はな hana flower

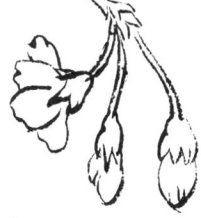
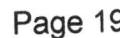

Lesson 1: Nouns, Numbers

1. You want to know what to call something in Japanese.

Point to objects and ask the teacher. If you learn more words, add them to the vocabulary list.

A: なんですか。 nan desu ka.	What is it?
B: ちずです。 chizu desu.	It's a map.

Substitute: dictionary, book, luggage, watch, ticket, paper, money

2. Vocabulary: Things used often

map	chizu	ちず
dictionary	jisho	じしょ
book	hon	ほん
pen	pen	ペン
paper	kami	かみ
money	okane	おかね
ticket	kippu	きっぷ
watch	tokei	とけい
luggage	nimotsu	にもつ
(ticket) to Tokyo	Tōkyō iki	とうきょう　いき

Grammar: nouns

a. Japanese nouns do not use articles (a, the). It is not necessary to specify singular or plural.
b. There is no distinction of gender.
c. Context makes it clear what is intended.

hon: book (a book, the book, books, the books)
sensei: teacher (a teacher, the teacher, teachers, the teachers)

Grammar: (noun) + desu : it's a (noun)

Desu is commonly translated: it is, I am, you are, he is, she is, they are, we are, etc.
In actual context there is no confusion about what is meant.

Hon desu.   It's a book. (They are books)
Sensei desu ka. Is it a teacher? (Are you a teacher? Is she the
                                  teacher? Are they teachers?)

Desu is used for polite speech. Without desu the sentence is abrupt, casual speech.

casual speech	polite speech	
Nani?	Nan desu ka.	What is it?
Okane?	Okane desu ka.	Is it money?
Ocha.	Ocha desu.	It is tea.
Tokyo.	Tokyo desu.	It is Tokyo.

Grammar: (sentence) + ka : question sentence

To make a question, add ka to a sentence.
There is no change of word order.

a. Pen desu ka.   Is it a pen?
   Pen desu.   It is a pen.
b. Nan desu ka.   What is it?
   Ocha desu.   It's tea.
c. Ikura desu ka.   How much is it?
   Sen en desu.   It's 1000 yen.

Page 21

3. Give the object that the teacher requests.
These sentences can be used at a store, restaurant.

A: ボブさん、　ペンを　ください。	
Bob san, <u>pen</u> o kudasai.	Please give me <u>a pen</u>, Bob.
B: どうぞ。	
Dōzo.	Here you are.

Substitute: paper, money, dictionary, map, clock, ticket

In many of the exercises in this book, you will have a chance to listen to the more complicated teacher's role, while you say the easier student's role. After several times, you will take the teacher's role. If you can't say it smoothly, it's too early for you to trade roles.

4. The teacher is wondering if it's a ticket.

A: きっぷ　ですか。	
<u>Kippu</u> desu ka.	Is it <u>a ticket?</u>
B: はい、そうです。	
Hai, sō desu.	Yes, it is.

Substitute: ticket, watch, luggage, map, money, tea

5. Give a negative answer to the teacher's guess.

A: とうきょう　いき　ですか。	
<u>Tōkyō iki</u> desu ka.	Is it <u>(a ticket) to Tokyo?</u>
B: いいえ、そうじゃ　ありません。	
Iie, sō ja arimasen.	No, it is not.

Substitute: ticket to Tokyo, map, dictionary, luggage, money, watch

Grammar: conjugation of (noun) + _desu_

1. affirmative: Tokyo desu.   It's Tokyo.
2. negative: Tokyo ja arimasen.   It isn't Tokyo.
3. past tense: Tokyo deshita.   It was Tokyo.
4. past negative: Tokyo ja arimasen deshita. It wasn't Tokyo.

6. Guessing game - what's hidden under the coat?

A: とけいですか。
   Tokei desu ka.
B: いいえ、そうじゃ ありません。
   Iie, sō ja arimasen.
A: じしょ ですか。
   Jisho desu ka.
B: はい、そうです。
   Hai, sō desu.

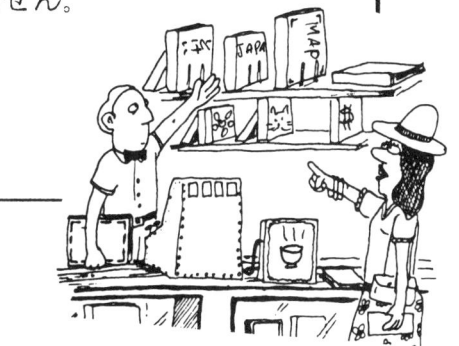

7. Vocabulary

this one	これ	kore
that one	それ	sore
that one over there	あれ	are
which one?	どれ	dore

8. Bring something in a bag to the teacher.

The bag is in front of the teacher.

A: これは なんですか。
   Kore wa nan desu ka.   What is this?
B: ほんです。
   Hon desu.   It's a book.

Substitute: pen, paper, watch, money, map, paper

9. This time the bag is near you, not in front of the teacher.

A: それは　なんですか。
   Sore wa nan desu ka.　　　　　　What is that?

B: これは　おかねです。
   Kore wa okane desu.　　　　　　This is money.

Substitute: ticket, watch, book, pen, dictionary

10. Put the bag in a corner of the room,..
not near you or the teacher.

A: あれは　なんですか。
   Are wa nan desu ka.　　What is that over there?

B: あれは　にもつです。
   Are wa nimotsu desu.　　That is Luggage over there.

Substitute: to Tokyo, map, money, watch, ticket, book

11. The teacher needs a dictionary. Which bag contains it?

A: じしょは　どれですか。
   Jisho wa dore desu ka.　　　　Which one is the dictionary?

B: これです・それです・あれです。
   Kore desu/Sore desu/Are desu.　　It's this/that/that over there.

Substitute: dictionary, watch, ticket, book, to Tokyo, map, money

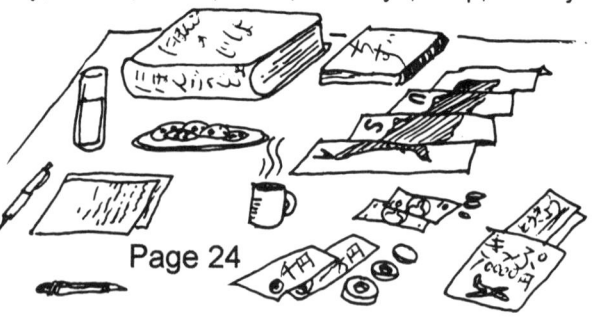

Grammar: (noun) + <u>wa</u> + (rest of sentence) : As for (noun) ...

<u>Wa</u> presents the theme of the sentence. It is similar to the concept of a subject in English. A literal translation into english is often unnatural and sometimes impossible. In this book the translations are as natural as possible.

Tokei wa sen en desu.   The watch is 1000 yen.
(lit. As for the watch, it's 1000 yen.)
Kippu wa ikura desu ka. How much is the ticket?
(lit. As for the ticket, how much is it?.)
Anata wa Bob san desu ka.   Are you Bob?
(lit. As for you, is it Bob?)

Grammar: omission of the "subject"

When the context is clear, a part of the sentence may be left off. Even the subject or object may be ommitted, in cases where this can not be done in English.

(Anata wa) Nihonjin desu ka.   (Are you) Japanese?
(Kore wa) nan desu ka.   What is (this)?
(Sore wa) chizu desu.   (That) is a map.

JANKEN PON   じゃんけん ぽん JANKEN PON

Before starting games, decide who is the first player, 2nd, 3rd,..... *JANKEN* is a simple way for establishing a winner and a loser. The two players shout,'janken pon!' and at the same time form their hands into shapes representing a stone (ishi), scissors (hasami), or paper (kami). A stone is stronger than scissors, scissors are stronger than paper, paper is stronger than a stone. If there is a tie, the chant is different. Say *aiko desho.* On the word *sho*, make one of the hand positions. The game goes on until there is a winner.

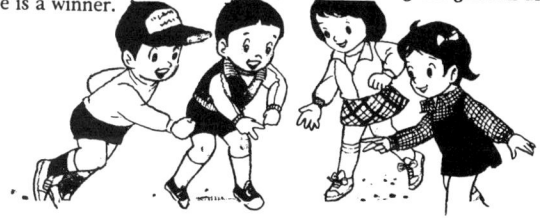

12. Act this out in class.

You are looking for something in a store. Practice this with various objects.

A: すみません。
Sumimasen.　　　　　　　　　Excuse me.
これは　じしょですか。
Kore wa jisho desu ka.　　　　Is this <u>a dictionary</u>?

B: そうじゃ　ありません。
Sō ja arimasen.　　　　　　　No, it is not.

A: じしょは　どれですか。
<u>Jisho</u> wa dore desu ka.　　　Which one is <u>a dictionary</u>?

B: あれです。
Are desu.　　　　　　　　　　That one over there.

A: あれを　ください。
Are o kudasai.　　　　　　　Please give me that over there.

B: はい、どうぞ。
Hai, dōzo.　　　　　　　　　Here you are.

A: ありがとう。
Arigatō.　　　　　　　　　　Thank you.

B: ありがとう　ございました。
Arigatō gozaimashita.　　　　Thank you.
また　どうぞ。
Mata dōzo.　　　　　　　　　Come back again.

Note: "arigatō gozaimashita" is grammatically the past tense of "arigatō gozaimasu". You can think of it as, "Thank you very much for what you have done."

13. Numbers

0 rei / zero	10 jū	20 nijū
れい・ぜろ	じゅう	にじゅう
1 ichi	11 juichi	21 niju ichi
いち	じゅういち	にじゅういち
2 ni	12 juni	22 niju ni
に	じゅうに	にじゅうに
3 san	13 jusan	30 sanjū
さん	じゅうさん	さんじゅう
4 shi / yon /yo	14 jushi	40 yonjū
し・よん・よ	じゅうし	よんじゅう
5 go	15 jugo	50 gojū
ご	じゅうご	ごじゅう
6 roku	16 juroku	60 rokujū
ろく	じゅうろく	ろくじゅう
7 shichi / nana	17 jushichi	70 shichijū
しち・なな	じゅうしち	しちじゅう
8 hachi	18 juhachi	80 hachijū
はち	じゅうはち	はちじゅう
9 ku / kyu	19 juku	90 kyujū
く・きゅう	じゅうく	きゅうじゅう

100 hyaku	200 nihyaku	300 sanbyaku
ひゃく	にひゃく	さんびゃく
1000 sen	2000 nisen	3000 sanzen
せん	にせん	さんぜん
10000 ichiman	20000 niman	30000 sanman
いちまん	にまん	さんまん

a. Big numbers are easy to figure out. Put a comma after the fourth number from the end of a number. Say man at the comma, then read the rest of the numbers : 532,7591 gohyaku sanju ni man shichi sen gohyaku kyuju ichi

b. Numbers were borrowed from ancient China. The alternate forms (yon) and (nana) are from the original Japanese numbers.

c. As a beginner, don't worry too much about the phonetic shifts such as san + hyaku = sanbyaku, or san + sen = sanzen.

d. If you listen to the tapes a few minutes every day, the correct forms will automatically sound "right" to you.

Page 27

14. What time?

Set your clock (made from paper) as the teacher tells you the time.

いま　ごじ　です。

Ima 5 ji desu.   Now it's 5 o'clock.

Substitute : 10, 12, 9, 7, 6, 8

15. Open your book to the page the teacher says.

にじゅうページを　あけて　ください

niju peji o akete kudasai.   Please open to page 20.

Substitute: page 90, page 60, page 100, page 374

16. Tell your telephone number.

A: でんわ　ばんごうは　なんばんですか。

Denwa bango wa nanban desu ka.   What is your tel. number?.

B: 253 の　4698です。

Ni go san no yon roku ku hachi desu.

Substitute: 781-3642,   590-3578,   302-5494, 206-9208

17. You are a bank teller.

Give the correct amount of play money to the teacher.

さんまんえん　おねがい　します。

San man en onegai shimasu.   May I have 30000 yen?

Substitute: 700 yen, 50 dollars, 1743 yen, 12300 dollars

18. Vocabulary: people, countries, languages

I / me	watashi	わたし
you	anata	あなた
teacher	sensei	せんせい
student	seito	せいと
student (high school, college)	gakusei	がくせい
bank worker	ginkōin	ぎんこういん
store clerk	ten-in	てんいん
friend	tomodachi	ともだち
Japan	Nihon	にほん
Japanese	Nihongo (language)	にほんご
Japanese	Nihonjin (person)	にほんじん
America	Amerika	アメリカ
English	Eigo (language)	えいご
American	Amerikajin (person)	アメリカじん

19. Vocabulary : question words

what	nani / nan	なに・なん
which	dore	どれ
who	dare	だれ
how much	ikura	いくら
where	doko	どこ

(noun 1) + no + (noun 2)

what book?	nan no hon	なんの ほん
book on tea	ocha no hon	おちゃの ほん
which book?	dono hon	どの ほん
this book	kono hon	この ほん
whose book?	dare no hon	だれの ほん
your book	anata no hon	あなたの ほん
what price book?	ikura no hon	いくらの ほん
100 yen book	100 en no hon	ひゃくえんの ほん
book from where?	doko no hon	どこの ほん
book from Japan	Nihon no hon	にほんの ほん

Grammar: (noun 1) + no + (noun 2) : (noun 1)'s (noun 2)

No is used when one noun modifies another noun. It is similar to "apostrophe-s", or to "of".

dare no nimotsu	whose luggage
watashi no nimotsu	my luggage
nan no hon	what book
ocha no hon	book of tea
ikura no hon	what price book
sen en no hon	1000 yen book
Nihongo no hon o kudasai.	Please give me the Japanese book
Tokyo iki no kippu o kudasai.	Please give me a ticket to Tokyo.
Kore wa Nihon no tokei desu.	This is a watch from Japan.

<u>When the context is clear, the second noun phrase may be left off.</u>

Kore wa dare no (hon) desu ka?	Whose (book) is this?
Are wa dare no desu ka.	Whose is that?
Watashi no desu.	It's mine.
Ju doru no (hon) o onegai shimasu.	May I have the $10 (book)?

20. The teacher is holding two books.

One is called Tea of Japan, 500 yen, written in Japanese, published in Japan and belongs to the teacher. The other is American Maps, 20 dollars, written in English, published in America and belongs to a friend.

A: おちゃの　ほんは　どれですか。
   Ocha no hon wa dore desu ka.　Which one is <u>a book on tea?</u>
B: それです。
   Sore desu.　　　　　　　　It's that one.

Substitute:
1. book on tea
2. book of maps
3. 500 yen book
4. 20 dollar book
5. my book
6. friend's book
7. book in Japanese
8. English book
9. book of Japan
10. American book

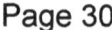

Page 30

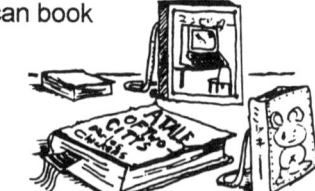

21. Use any words you know to ask about things in the room.

A: ボブさんの　にもつは　どれですか。
Bob san no nimotsu wa dore desu ka.　Which is Bob's luggage?

B: それです。Sore desu.　　　　　That one.

Substitute: my Japanese dictionary, your ticket to Tokyo

22. Give the book the teacher asks for.

わたしの　ほんを　ください。
Watashi no hon o kudasai.　　　Please give me my book.

Substitute: $20 book, Japanese book, English book, your book

23. The teacher wants to buy something from you.
Look at the price tag and read the price.

A: アメリカの　ほんは　いくらですか。
Amerika no hon wa ikura desu ka. How much is the American book?
B: にじゅうドルです。
20 doru desu.　　　　It's 20 dollars.

Substitute: book from Japan, your pen, English book, 10 yen book

24. Identify the owner of something the teacher has.

A: これは　だれの　ほんですか。
Kore wa dare no hon desu ka. Whose book is this?

B: せんせいの　ほんです。
Sensei no hon desu.　　　It's the teacher's book.

Substitute: money-Bob's, ticket-Ann's, watch-mine

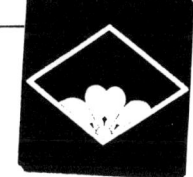

Page 31

Variation

Identify the owner of various things in the room. Use kore/sore/are depending on the location.

25. Identify the subject of various books.

A: それは　なんの　ほんですか。
Sore wa nan no hon desu ka.　　　　What book is that?

B: おちゃの　ほんです。
Ocha no hon desu.　　　　It's a book on tea.

Substitute: book of maps, book on flowers (hana), book on Japan

26. Ask about various things which are;
close to you, close to the listener, or far away.

A これは　アメリカの　とけいですか。
Kore wa Amerika no tokei desu ka.　　Is this an American watch?
B: はい、アメリカの　です。
Hai, Amerika no desu.　　　　Yes, it's American.
　　いいえ、アメリカの　じゃ　ありません。
Iie, Amerika no ja arimasen.　　　　No, it's not American.

Substitute: friend's luggage, 500 yen book, my paper, book about me

27. The teacher is asking about something you bought.

A: にほんごの　ほんは　いくらでしたか。
Nihongo no hon wa ikura deshita ka.
　　　　　　　　　　How much was the Japanese book?
B: にじゅうドル　でした。
Niju doru deshita.　　It was 20 dollars.

Substitute: American watch - $40, Japanese dictionary - 1000 yen

Page 32

28. Dialog 1

Bob has just arrived at Narita Airport (Narita Kuko) in Tokyo.

B: すみません。あなたは　もり　みちよさんですか。
Sumimasen.　Anata wa <u>Mori Michiyo</u> san desu ka.

M: はい、そうです。あなたは　ボブさんですか。
Hai, sō desu.　Anata wa <u>Bob</u> san desu ka.

B: はい、そうです。どうぞ　よろしく。
Hai, sō desu.　Dōzo yoroshiku.

M: みちよです。どうぞ　よろしく。
<u>Michiyo</u> desu.　Dōzo yoroshiku.

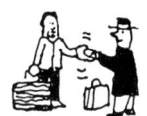

29. Dialog 2

M: ボブさんの　にもつは　どれですか。
<u>Bob</u> san no <u>nimotsu</u> wa dore desu ka.

B: すみません。わかりません。
　もういちど　いって　ください。
Sumimasen.　Wakarimasen.　Mō ichido itte kudasai.

M: ボブさんの　にもつは　どれですか。
<u>Bob</u> san no nimotsu wa dore desu ka.

B: あ、わかりました。わたしのは　あれです。
A, wakarimashita.　Watashi no wa are desu.

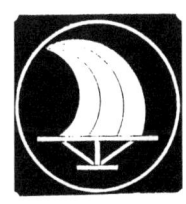

30. Dialog 3 (B: Bob, C: clerk)
Bob's first experience of shopping in a Japanese store.

B: ごめん　ください。　　　Gomen kudasai.

C: いらっしゃいませ。　　　Irasshai mase.

B: とうきょうの　ちずは　いくらですか。

　　　　　　　　　　　Tōkyō no chizu wa ikura desu ka.

C: えいごのは　ごひゃくえんです。

　　　　　　　　　　　Eigo no wa gohyaku en desu.

B: にほんごのは?　　　　　Nihongo no wa?

C: にひゃくえんです。　　　Niihyaku en desu.

B: にほんごのを　おねがいします。

　　　　　　　　　　　Nihongo no o onegai shimasu.

　　はい、にひゃくえん、どうぞ。Hai, nihyaku en.　Dozo.

C: あ、これは　にほんの　おかねじゃ　ありません。

　　　　　　　　　　　A, kore wa Nihon no okane ja arimasen.

　　どこの　ですか。　　Doko no desu ka.

B: すみません。これは　アメリカのです。

　　　　　　　　　　　Sumimasen. Kore wa Amerika no desu.

　　にほんのを　どうぞ。Nihon no o dōzo.

C: ありがとう　ございます。また　どうぞ。

　　　　　　　　　　　Arigato gozaimasu. mata dozo.

31. Vocabulary : Daily objects, useful expressions

name	namae	なまえ
tea	ocha	おちゃ
telephone	denwa	でんわ
telephone number	denwa bangō	でんわばんごう
flower	hana	はな
-o'clock	-ji	ーじ
-yen	-en	ーえん
a few	chotto	ちょっと
again	mata	また
once again	mō ichido	もう　いちど
please	dōzo	どうぞ
sorry	sumimasen	すみません
not understand	wakarimasen	わかりません

LET'S PRACTICE SOME MORE.
もっと れんしゅう しましょう。
See introductory lesson for details.

<u>Vocabulary builders</u>
1. Make cards   2. Listen and stand up

3. Listen and line up   4. Spread on the table

5. Shoots and ladders   6. Around the world

<u>Quick draw + Full house bingo</u>

<u>Expressions</u>

1. Sensei no tokei wa Nihon no desu.
2. Are wa Eigo no jisho desu.
3. Tomodachi no Tokyo iki no kippu wa sen en desu.
4. Nihongo no sensei wa Nihonjin ja arimasen.
5. Anata no chizu wa kore desu.
6. Kore wa denwa no hon desu.
7. Sore wa tenin no nimotsu desu.
8. Ocha no hon wa hyaku en ja arimasen.
9. Watashi wa Tokyo no ginkoin deshita.

<u>Change positive and negative</u>
Change positive sentences to negative and negative to positive.

a. Nimotsu desu.
b. Kore wa kami ja arimasen.
c. Sore wa ocha desu.
d. Are wa Tokyo iki ja arimasen.
e. Okane desu.
f. Watashi wa tenin deshita.
g. Tokyo iki wa 1000 en ja arimasen deshita.

Page 35

Match English - Japanese

a. What is that over there?　じしょは　どれですか。
b. Please give me a book.　これは　きっぷですか。
c. Is this a ticket?　それは　とけいじゃ　ありません。
d. That is not a clock.　あれは　なんですか。
e. Which is a dictionary?　ほんを　ください。
f. Were you a student?　せんせいは　だれですか。
g. This was not a book.　きっぷを　おねがいします。
h. May I have a ticket?　これは　ほんじゃ　ありませんでした。
i. Who is the teacher?　あなたは　がくせいでしたか。

Matchng: B's response to A

1.

A	B
a. Sore wa nan desu ka.	a. Sensei no desu.
b. Are wa kippu desu ka.	b. Are desu.
c. Chizu wa dore desu ka.	c. Kore wa tokei desu.
d. Anata wa Michiyo san desu ka.	d. Iie, watashi wa Ann desu.
e. kore wa dare no kami desu ka.	e. Hai, are wa kippu desu.

2.

A	B
a. Tokei wa ikura deshita ka.	a. Gausei no desu.
b. Tokyo iki wa dore desu ka.	b. gojū en deshita.
c. Sore wa dare no desu ka.	c. Ocha no desu.
d. Kore wa nan no hon desu ka.	d. Amerika desu.
e. Nimotsu wa doko desu ka.	e. Are desu.

Two way bingo
1. On a 4 x 4 bingo grid sheet, write English words in the top row and the left column. Choose the words from the list. Fill the words in random order so that you avoid to make identical bingo game sheet.
2. The game leader says a basic sentence, substituting words chosen from the list. Mark the spot where two words meet.
3. The winner says the three sentences in a row.

Basic sentences
1. <u>Kore</u> wa watashi no <u>okane</u> desu.   <u>This</u> is my <u>money.</u>
    a   b

    a. this, that, that one over there
    b. money, luggage, map, ticket, watch

    Example sentences:

    1. Are wa watashi no tokei desu.
    2. Sore wa watashi no nimotsu desu.
    3. Kore wa watashi no kippu desu.
    4. Sore wa watashi no chizu desu.
    5. Are wa watashi no okane desu.

2. <u>Chizu</u> wa <u>100</u> en deshita.   The map was 100 yen.

    a. dictionary, watch, paper, telephone, book
    b. 100, 300, 4000, 5000, 60000

3. <u>Nihongo no jisho</u> wa <u>watashi</u> no ja arimasen.
    The Japanese dictionary is not mine.

    a. Japanese map, Japanese money,
       English dictionary, American ticket
    b. mine, yours, teacher's, student's, my friend'

Guessing game

Guess what's the answer. Ask using the basic sentence.
Substitute a possible answer from the words listed.

1. Sore wa <u>tokei</u> desu ka.
     <u>Possible answer:</u>
        watch, map, Japanese book, English dictionary, ticket, pen

2. Ima <u>6ji</u> desu ka.

     7, 9, 11, 12, 5, 3, 6

3. Are wa <u>10</u> yen desu ka.

     20, 30, 40, 60, 70, 90

4. Anata wa <u>sensei</u> deshita ka.

     teacher, student, English teacher, clerk, bank worker, friend

5. Kore wa <u>ocha</u> no hon desu ka.

     map, English, Japanese, clock, telephone, Japanese money

6. Kore wa <u>tenin</u> no nimotsu desu ka.

     student, English teacher, Japanese, I, you, American, friend

7. Sore wa <u>gakusei</u> no desu ka.

     English teacher, you, American, friend, Japanese, I

8. Tokyo iki no kippu wa <u>100 en</u> desu ka.

     200, 300, 400, 500, 600, 700, 800

9. Anata no tokei wa <u>1000 en</u> deshita ka.

     2000, 3000, 4000, 7000, 8000, 9000

About myself
1. Which sentences are true about yourself?
2. Write about yourself.
3. Speech presentation: Tell about yourself.

1. Watashi wa Nihonjin desu.
2. Watashi no sensei wa Nihonjin desu.
3. Watashi no tomodachi wa Amerikajin ja arimasen.
4. Watashi wa ginkōin deshita.
5. Watashi wa tenin ja arimasen deshita.
6. Watashi no denwa bangō wa 132 no 8906 desu.
7. Watashi no tokei wa Amerika no desu.
8. Watashi wa genki ja arimasen.
9. Watashi no okane wa Nihon no desu.
10. Watashi no jisho wa Nihongo ja arimasen.

Interview

Example questionnaire

1. Sore wa nan desu ka.
2. Sumimasen. Chizu o kudasai.
3. Are wa nan desu ka.
4. Sore wa okane desu ka.
5. Kore wa Tokyo iki desu ka, Ōsaka iki desu ka.
6. Nimotsu wa dore desu ka.
7. Anata no namae wa nan desu ka
8. Kore wa 100 en deshita ka.
9. Anata no denwa bangō wa nan ban desu ka.
10. Ima 9 ji desu ka.
11. 1000 en onegai shimasu.
12. Party wa nan ji desu ka.

Constructing a sentence
Write good sentences using all the parts.

1. Please give me a dictionary.
   じしょ、　　くださ　い、　　を

2. What is that over there?
   です、あれ、なん、か、は

3. Which one is the luggage?
   か、どれ、にもつ、は、です

4. This is not a ticket.
   これ、じゃ、きっぷ、ありません、は

5. Which one is my money?
   おかね、です、どれ、か、わたし、の、は

6. How much is a Japanese book?
   です、いくら、ほん、の、にほん、か、は

7. What book is that?
   か、ほん、なん、の、それ、は、です

8. This is not yours.
   じゃ、あなたの、ありません、これ、は

9. How much was English teacher's ticket?
   えいご、か、は、いくら、せんせい、
   でした、の、の、きっぷ

A letter to your pen pal

Write a letter to your pen pal in Japanese and English.
Tell about you. Ask about your pen pal.

Example:

ボブさん、こんにちは。おげんきですか。
わたしは　げんきです。
わたしは　にほんじんです。
アメリカじんじゃ　ありません。
えいごの　がくせいです。
えいごの　せんせいは　にほんじんじゃ　ありません。
アメリカじんです。
せんせいは　ぎんこういんでした。
ボブさんは　にほんごの　がくせいですか。
あなたは　てんいんでしたか。
わたしの　ともだちは　てんいんでした。
ともだちは　ひろしさんです。
ボブさんの　でんわばんごうは　なんばんですか。
わたしのは　５３１の９７４３です。
ボブさん、アメリカの　ちずを　ください。
　　　　　　　さようなら　　　みちよ　より

Answer the questions from the letter.

1. Kore wa dare no tegami (letter) desu ka.
2. Michiyo san wa genki desu ka, genki ja arimasen ka.
3. Michiyo san wa Amerika jin desu ka.
4. Michiyo san wa nan no gakusei deu ka.
5. Eigo no sensei wa nani jin desu ka.
6. Sensei wa nan deshita ka.
7. Michiyo san no tomodachi wa nan deshita ka.
8. Michiyo san no tomodachi wa dare desu ka.
9. 531 no 9743 wa dare no denwa bangō desu ka.

Write a letter to a pen pal.

Evaluation : Listening comprehension

1.
a. Which is it?
b. How much is it?
c. Who are you?
d. Where is it?

6.
a. It's 5 o'clock.
b. It isn't 5 o'clock.
c. It was 5 o'clock.
d. It wasn't 5 o'clock.

2.
a. What is it?
b. What book is it?
c. Whose book is it?
d. How much is the book?

7.
a. Which is your luggage?
b. Which is my luggage?
c. Where is your luggage?
d. Where is my luggage?

3.
a. This is a ticket.
b. That is a ticket.
c. Is this a ticket?
d. Is that a ticket?

8.
a. Whose flower is it?
b. Whose ticket is it?
c. Whose dictionary is it?
d. Whose watch is it?

4.
a. It's my paper.
b. It was my paper.
c. It isn't my paper.
d. It wasn't my paper.

9.
a. What ticket is it?
b. What watch is it?
c. What book is it?
d. What dictionary is it?

5.
a. Give me the map.
b. May I have the map?
c. Where is the map?
d. Which is the map?

10.
a. This is the teacher's.
b. That is yours.
c. That over there is mine.
d. Which is my friend's?

Evaluation: Speaking 1

Evaluation: Speaking 2

Scoring guide: date   name

a. Vocabulary: variety, new words	0 1 2 3 4
b. Sentence: variety, new structures	0 1 2 3 4
c. Attitude: gesture, eye contact	0 1 2 3 4
d. Voice: clear and natural	0 1 2 3 4
e. Memorized?	0 1 2 3 4

Your total points   / 20

Evaluation: Reading and writing

1. Where is my luggage?
   (   ) の (   ) は　どこですか。

2. This is not your paper.
   (   ) は　あなたの　かみ (   )。

3. Who is an English teacher?
   (   ) のせんせいは (   ) ですか。

4. Bob was a Japanese student.

   ボブさんは (   ) のがくせい (   )。

5. Ann was not a store clerk.
   アンさんは　てんいん (   )。

6. What book is that over there?
   あれは (   ) のほんですか。

7. Which is your friend's book?
   あなたの (   ) のほんは (   ) ですか。

8. How much was the book on flowers?
   (   ) のほんは (   ) でしたか。

Page 43

Lesson 2: Places and Transportation

1. Your teacher is a stranger in town who needs direction.

There are signs or pictures posted around the room representing the places listed below. Point out the place while giving directions.

A: <u>Annaisho</u> wa doko desu ka.	Where's <u>the information center?</u>
あんないしょは　どこですか。	
B: <u>Asoko</u> desu.	It's over there.
あそこです。	

Substitute: train station, bus stop, airport, store, bank, town

2. Vocabulary: places

information center	annaisho	あんないしょ
train station	eki	えき
bus stop	basu noriba	バスのりば
airport	kūkō	くうこう
restroom, toilet	otearai, benjo, toire	おてあらい
		べんじょ、トイレ
inn	ryokan	りょかん
bank	ginkō	ぎんこう
post office	yūbinkyoku	ゆうびんきょく
store	mise	みせ
restaurant	resutoran	レストラン
friend's house	tomodachi no ie	ともだちの　いえ

Ask about each other's homes.

<u>Bob</u> san no ie wa doko desu ka.　Where's <u>Bob's</u> home?
ボブさんの　いえは　どこですか。

3. Vocabulary: location pronouns

this place, here	koko	ここ
that place, there	soko	そこ
that place over there	asoko	あそこ
which place, where	doko	どこ

4. Pictures: your teacher stands in front of the signs posted
around the room and asks,

A: Koko wa kūkō desu ka. ここは　くうこうですか。	Is this the airport?
B: Hai, kūkō desu. はい、くうこうです。	Yes, it's the airport.
(or)	
Hai, sō desu. はい、そうです。	Yes, it is.

Substitute: restroom, inn, friend's house, post office, airport, bank

5. You are holding a sign representing a place.
The teacher asks about it but guesses wrong.

A: Soko wa ginkō desu ka. そこは　ぎんこうですか。	Is that a bank?
B: Iie, ginkō ja arimasen. いいえ、ぎんこうじゃ　ありません。	No, it's not a bank.
(or)	
Iie, sō ja arimasen. いいえ、そうじゃありません。	No, it's not.

Substitute: post office, store, bus stop, station, inn

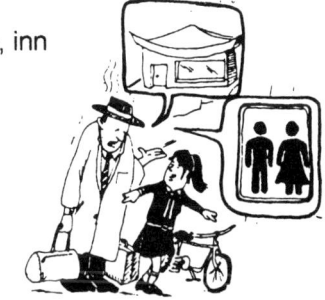

Page 45

6. The teacher is wondering what that place over there is.

A: Asoko wa <u>resutoran</u> desu ka.   Is that <u>a restaurant</u> over there?
　あそこは　レストランですか。

B: Iie, <u>resutoran</u> ja arimasen..   No, it's not <u>a restaurant</u>..
　いいえ、レストランじゃ　ありません。
　<u>Ginko</u> desu.   It's <u>a bank.</u>
　ぎんこうです。

Substitute: friend's house - my house, information center - station, inn - store, bank - post office, airport - information booth

7. Act this out in class.
Try looking for other places too.

A: Sumimasen, Koko wa <u>ryokan</u> desu ka.
　すみません。ここは　りょかんですか。

B: Iie, <u>ryokan</u> ja arimasen.
　いいえ、りょかんじゃ　ありません。

A: <u>Ryokan</u> wa doko desu ka.
　りょかんは　どこですか。

B: Asoko desu.
　あそこです。

A: Dōmo arigatō gozaimasu.
　どうも　ありがとう　ございます。

B: Iie.
　いいえ。

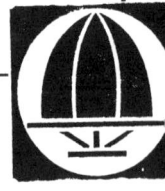

8. Your teacher invites you to go to various places.

Get up and walk over to pictures or signs posted around the room.

Ann san, issho ni <u>yama</u> e ikimashō.

アンさん、いっしょに　やまへ　いきましょう。

Ann, let's go to <u>the mountain</u> together.

Kaerimashō.   Let's return home.

かえりましょう。

Substitute: sea, hotsprings, castle, temple, airport, company

Grammar: (place) + e + (verb): to, towards

to school	gakko e
I go to school	Watashi wa gakko e ikimasu.
Students came to Japan.	Gakusei wa Nihon e kimashita.
Where did you go?	Doko e ikimashita ka.

Grammar: (verb stem) + masu

ikimasu : iki (stem) + masu (ending)

Verb conjugation:

go / will go (future)	ikimasu	いきます
don't go (negative)	ikimasen	いきません
went (past)	ikimashita	いきました
didn't go	ikimasen deshita	いきません　でした
let's go	ikimashō	いきましょう
Shall I / we go?	ikimashō ka	いきましょうか

Examples:

Sensei wa Nihon e ikimasu.	The teacher will go to Japan.
Basu de kaerimasu.	I return home by bus.
Watashi wa kaerimasen.	I won't go home.
Bob san wa kimasen deshita.	Bob didn't come.
Kaerimashō.	Let's go home.
Doko e ikimashō ka.	Where shall we go?
Ashita koko e kimashō ka.	Shall I come here tomorrow?

9. Vocabulary : places

mountain	yama	やま
sea	umi	うみ
hotspring	onsen	おんせん
island	shima	しま
temple	otera	おてら
castle	oshiro	おしろ
town	machi	まち
school	gakkō	がっこう
company	kaisha	かいしゃ

Grammar: word order

Word order of Japanese sentence is different from English.
The verb comes at the end of the sentence. Other than that, the
word order varies considerably. The subject is not always first.

1, Sensei wa Nihon e ikimasu.　　　　　The teacher goes to Japan.
   Nihon e sensei wa ikimasu.
2, Tomodachi wa gakkō e ikimashita ka. Did the friend go to school?
   Gakkō e tomodachi wa ikimashita ka.
3, Issho ni mise e ikimashō ka.　　　Shall we go to the store together?
   Mise e issho ni ikimashō ka.
4, Nihonjin wa machi e ikimasen. The Japanese don't go to town.
   Machi e nihonjin wa ikimasen.
5, Tenin wa mise e kaerimasen deshita.　　The clerk didn't return
   Mise e tenin wa kaerimasen deshita.　　to the store..
6, Bob san wa Amerika e kimasu ka.　Does Bob come to America?
   Amerika e Bob san wa kimasu ka.

10. Your teacher invites you to go somewhere.

A: Ima <u>shima</u> e ikimashō ka.   Shall we go to <u>the island</u> now?
いま　しまへ　いきましょうか。

B: Hai, issho ni ikimashō.   Yes, let's go together.
はい、いっしょに　いきましょう。

Substitute: temple, castle, company, school, town, airport, inn

11. Your teacher is ready to show you around.

A: Ann san, doko e ikimashō ka.   Where shall we go, Ann?
アンさん、どこへ　いきましょうか。

B: <u>Machi</u> e ikimashō.   Let's go to <u>town.</u>
まちへ　いきましょう。

Substitute: school, company, friend's house, airport, temple, station

12. Your teacher asks about your daily routine.

The form <u>ikimasu</u> can be used for a simple present tense - something that usually happens.

A: Mainichi <u>kaisha</u> e ikimasu ka.   Do you go to <u>the company</u>
まいにち　かいしゃへ　いきますか。 every day?

B: Hai, mainichi ikimasu.   Yes, I go every day.
はい、まいにち　いきます。

Substitute: school, town, bus stop, temple, station, airport, inn

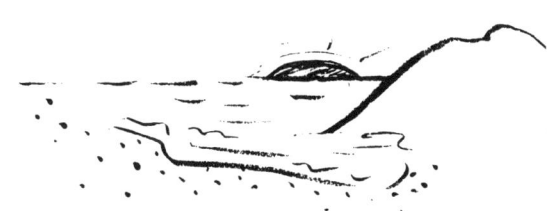

13. Your teacher asks about tomorrow's plans.

Ikimasu can also be used for future tense.

A: Bob san wa ashita doko e ikimasu ka.
　ボブさんは　あした　どこへ　いきますか。
　　　　　　　　　　Where will you go tomorrow, Bob?
B: Yama e ikimasu.　　　I will go to the mountain.
　やまへ　いきます。

Substitute:sea, hotspring, school, town, temple, friend's house

14. Now the teacher is asking about what you did yesterday.

Ikimashita is the past tense.

A: Ann san wa kinō doko e ikimashita ka.
　アンさんは　きのう　どこへ　いきましたか。
　　　　　　　　　　Where did you go yesterday, Ann?
B: Shima e ikimashita.　　I went to the island.
　しまへ　いきました。

Substitute: temple, castle, school, town, bank, Bob's town

15. Tell the teacher whether or not you will go tomorrow.

Ikimasen is the negative.

A: Ashita machi e ikimasu ka. Will you go to town tomorrow, or not?
　あした　まちへ　いきますか。

B: Ikimasen..　　　　　　I won't go.
　いきません。

Substitute: temple, school, company, castle, town, station

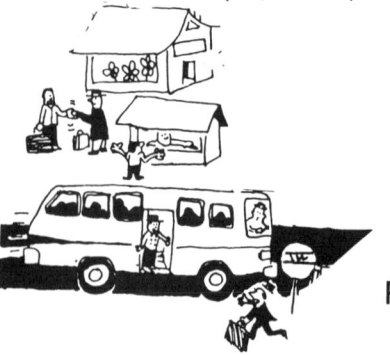

16. The teacher wants to know if you went yesterday.

A: Kinō umi e ikimashita ka.   Did you go to the sea yesterday or
きのう　うみへ　いきましたか。   not?

S: Ikimasen deshita..   I didn't go.
いきません　でした。

Substitute: hotsprings, island, your company, the teacher's house

17. Pattern drill: Tomorrow and Yesterday

A: Ahita ikimasu ka.   Will you go tomorrow?
あした　いきますか。

B: Ikimasen.   I won't go.
いきません。

A: Kinō ikimashita ka.   Did you go yesterday?
きのう　いきましたか。

B: Ikimasen deshita.   I didn't go.
いきません　でした。

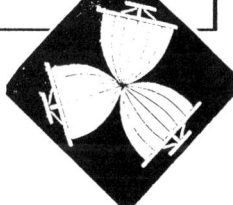

Substitute: go, come, return, travel, do

18. Act this out in class.
You are travelling together in Japan and deciding where to go next.
Practice this with other places, too.

A: Kyo, doko e ikimashō ka.   Where shall we go today?
きょう、どこへ　いきましょうか。

B: Oshiro e ikimashō ka.   Shall we go to the castle?
おしろへ　いきましょうか。

A:: Watashi wa kinō ikimashita. I went there yesterday.
わたしは　きのう　いきました。

B: Jā, kyō wa umi e ikimashō.   Then, let's go to the sea today.
じゃ、きょうは　うみへ　いきましょう。

A: Sō shimashō.   Let's do that.
そう　しましょう。

19. Now that you've decided where to go, will you go by bus,...
by train, on foot? Take a card representing the vehicle the teacher
says, and act out going together.

> A: Bob san, <u>basu</u> de Tōkyō e ikimashō ka.
> ボブさん、バスで　とうきょうへ　いきましょうか。
> Shall we go to Tokyo <u>by bus,</u> Bob?
> B: Hai, sō shimashō.　　　Yes, let's do that.
> はい、そう　しましょう。

Substitute: taxi, car, bicycle, airplane, on foot, my car, your boat

Grammar: Particle <u>de</u> :　by means of, with, using

Basu de kimasu.	I come by bus.
Nani de Nihon e ikimashita ka.	How did you go to Japan?
Mainichi aruite kaerimasyō.	Let's return on foot every day.
Pen de kaite kudasai.	Please write with a pen.

20. Vocabulary : Transportation

bus	basu	バス
taxi	takushii	タクシー
car	kuruma	くるま
train	densha	でんしゃ
"Bullet Train"	shinkansen	しんかんせん
airplane	hikōki	ひこうき
ship	hune	ふね
bicycle	jitensha	じてんしゃ．
walking	aruite	あるいて

(<u>aruite</u> is not followed by <u>de</u>)

21. Tell how you go to town.

A: Itsumo nani de <u>machi</u> e ikimasu ka.
いつも　なにで　まちへ　いきますか。
How do you get to <u>town</u>?
B: <u>Densha</u> de ikimasu.   I go by <u>train</u>.
でんしゃで　いきます。

Substitute: ship, train, Bullet Train, bicycle, on foot, my bicycle

22. And how did you get here? How will you return home?
Kimasu means "I come"

A: Nani de koko e kimashita ka?	How did you come here?
なにで　ここへ　きましたか。	
B: <u>Basu</u> de kimashita.	I came by <u>bus.</u>
バスで　きました。	
A: Nani de kaerimasu ka.	How will you return home?
なにで　かえりますか。	
B: <u>Takushii</u> de kaerimasu.	I'll go home by <u>taxi.</u>
タクシーで　かえります。	

Substitute: car - ship, train - bicycle, on foot - airplane

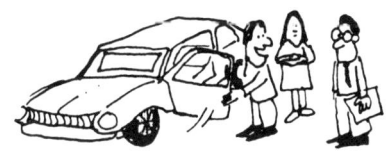

Grammar: (noun 1) + <u>to</u> + (noun 2)   Joining two nouns

hon to pen	a book and pen
hon to pen to kami	a book, a pen and paper
Hon to pen o kudasai.	Please give me a book and a pen.
Gakkō to mise e ikimasu.	I go to school and a store.
Party wa 5ji to 9ji desu.	The party is at 5 o'clock and 9 o'clock.
Tomodachi to issho ni kaerimasu.	I return with a friend.
Sensei to gakusei wa doko desu ka.	
	Where are the teachers and students?
Kuruma to densha de kite kudasai.	
	Please come by a car and a train.
100 en to 10 en o onegai shimasu.	
	May I have 100 yen and 10 yen?

23. Now you are in Japan.

It would be nice to have actual pamphlets from a travel agency and learn the names of places. Where shall we visit today?

A: <u>Yama</u> to <u>umi</u> e ikimashō ka.
やまと　うみへ　いきましょうか。
　　　　　　　　Shall we go to <u>the mountains</u> and <u>the sea</u>?
B: Hajime ni <u>yama</u> e ikimashō.   First let's go to <u>the mountains.</u>
　Sorekara <u>umi</u> e ikimashō.   Then let's go to <u>the sea.</u>
はじめに　やまへ　いきましょう。
それから　うみへ　いきましょう。

Substitute: town - mountain, hotspring - Tokyo, inn - bank

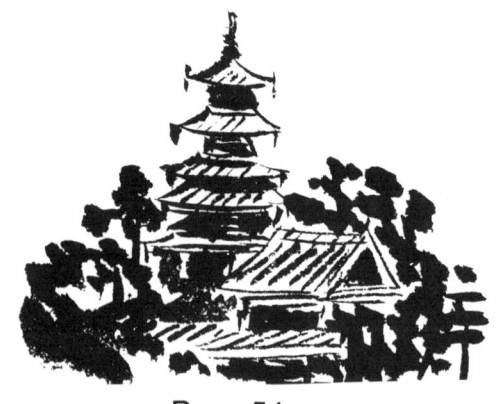

24. Ask about the teacher's recent trip.

A: Watashi wa ryokō shimashita.   I took a trip.
　わたしは　りょこう　しました。

B: <u>Otera</u> to <u>oshiro</u> e ikimashita ka.
　おてらと　おしろへ　いきましたか。
                 Did you go to <u>temples</u> and <u>castles</u>?

A: <u>Otera</u> e ikimashita ga, <u>oshiro</u> e ikimasen deshita.
　おてらへ　いきましたが、
　おしろへ　いきません　でした。
          I went to <u>temples</u>, but I didn't go to <u>castles</u>.

Substitute: town - mountain, hotsprings - Tokyo, island - sea

Grammar: (sentence 1) + ga + (sentence 2) : but

Ga is used to join two contrasting sentences.

    Umi e ikimasu ga yama e ikimasen.
                 I'll go to the sea, but not to the mountain.
    Nihonjin wa kimashita ga Amerikajin wa kimasen deshita.
                 The Japanese came, but the American didn't come.
    Aruite koko e kimasu ga takushii de kaerimasu.
                 I came here on foot, but I will return by taxi.
    Bob san wa sensei desu ga Ann san wa gakusei desu.
                 Bob is a teacher, but Ann is a student.
    Hon wa 100 en desu ga pen wa 100 en ja arimasen.
                 The book is 100 yen, but the pen is not 100 yen.

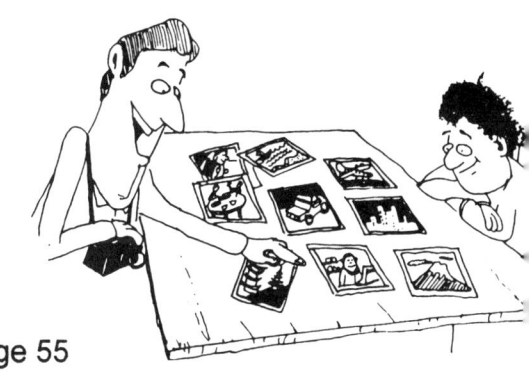

Page 55

25. Dialog 1

Michiyo is spending a few days showing Bob the sights. They are planning what to do tomorrow.

A: <u>Bob</u> san, ashita issho ni <u>oshiro</u> e ikimashō ka.
　ボブさん、あした　いっしょに　おしろへ
　いきましょうか。

B: Ii desu ne.
　いいですね。

A: <u>Shinkansen</u> de ikimashō.
　しんかんせんで　いきましょう。

B: <u>Oshiro</u> wa doko desu ka.
　おしろは　どこですか。

A: Chotto matte kudasai.
　ちょっと　まって　ください。
　Nihon no chizu wa doko desu ka.
　にほんの　ちずは　どこですか。

B: Koko desu.
　ここです。

A: <u>Oshiro</u> wa koko desu.
　おしろは　ここです。

Answer the questions.

1. Bob san wa ashita doko e ikimasu ka.
2. Nani de oshiro e ikimasu ka.
3. Nihon no chizu wa doko desu ka.

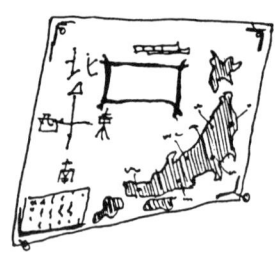

26. Dialog 2
Bob is talking with Michiyo's friend Ann.

A: <u>Bob</u> san wa mainichi Nihongo no gakkō e ikimasu ka.
　ボブさんは　まいにち　にほんごの　がっこうへ
　いきますか。
B: Taitei ikimasu ga, kinō wa ikimasen deshita.
　たいてい　いきますが、　きのうは
　いきません　でした。
A: Doko e ikimashita ka.
　どこへ　いきましたか。
B: <u>Michiyo</u> san to issho ni <u>oshiro</u> e ikimashita.
　みちよさんと　いっしょに　おしろへ　いきました。

Answer the questions.
1. Bob san wa mainichi doko e ikimasu ka.
2. Kinō, Bob san wa Nihongo no gakkō e ikimashita ka.
3. Michiyo san wa dare to oshiro e ikimashita ka.

27. Vocabulary

go	ikimasu	いきます
come	kimasu	きます
return	kaerimasu	かえります
do	shimasu	します
travel	ryokō shimasu	りょこう　します
now	ima	いま
every day	mainichi	まいにち
today	kyō	きょう
tomorrow	ashita	あした
yesterday	kinō	きのう
usually	taitei	たいてい
sometimes	tokidoki	ときどき
always	itsumo	いつも
together	issho ni	いっしょに
first	hajime ni	はじめに
then	sore kara	それから
good	ii	いい

LET'S PRACTICE SOME MORE.
もっと　れんしゅう　しましょう。
See Introductory lesson for details.

Vocabulary builders
1. Make cards
2. Listen and stand up
3. Listen and line up
4. Spread on the table
5. Shoots and ladders
6. Around the world

Quick draw + Full house bingo

Expressions

1. Gakusei to ginkōin wa aruite umi to yama e ikimasu.
2. Mainichi tenin wa jitensha to aruite ie e kaerimasu.
3. Sensei wa kinō kaisha e ikimashita ga kaeriimasen deshita.
4. Kyō tomodachi wa nihon no kuruma de ocha no mise e ikimasu.
5. Eigo no sensei wa Nihongo no gakusei no ie e kimashita.
6. Kinō Bob san wa asoko e ikimashita.
7. Ashita koko e kimasu.
8. Nihonjin to issho ni ryokō shimashita.
9. Kinō tenin wa mise e ikimasen deshita.

Change positive and negative.

1. Watashi wa Nihon e ikimasu.
2. Tomodachi wa ashita koko e kimasen.
3. Sensei wa gakkō e kaerimasen.
4. Ginkōin wa kuruma de ryokō shimashita.
5. Nihonjin wa hune de ryokō shimasen deshita.
6. Gakusei wa sensei to issho ni gakkō e kimashita.
7. Watashi wa tomodachi to issho ni machi e ikimasen deshita.

Fill in ( ).

Choose from: de, no, ka, to, ga, e, wa

a. joining two contransting sentences: (   )
b. by means of, with, using: (   )
c. to, towards: (   )
d. joining two nouns, and: (   )
e. question marker: (   )
f. theme, as for-: (   )
g. of, modifier, apostrophe-s: (   )

Choose one.

1. Sensei wa kuruma (to / de / ka) koko e kimashita.
2. Watashi (e / no / wa) tomodachi wa densha de kaerimashita.
3. Nihonjin wa Amerika (de / wa / e) kimasu.
4. Mise e ikimasu (no / ga / de) yama e ikimasen.
5. Kino eki (de / e / to) annaisho e ikimashita.

Matching: B's response to A

A	B
a. Doko e ikimashō ka.	a. Tenin to issho ni ikimasu.
b. Nani de koko e kimashita ka.	b. Onsen e ikimashō.
c. Nihon e ryokō shimashita ka.	c. Iie, jitensha de kaerimasu.
d. Mainichi aruite kaerimasu ka.	d. Hune de kimashita.
e. Dare to issho ni machi e ikimasu ka.	e. Hai, ryokō shimashita.

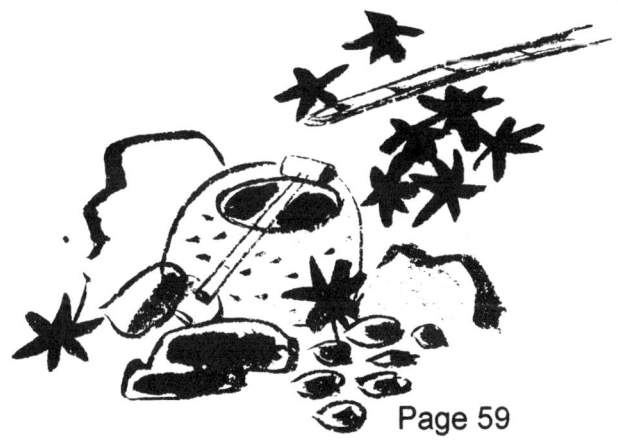

Two way bingo

Basic sentences   Preparation: Fill in words for substituting.

1. Mainichi gakusei wa eki e ikimasu. Sensei wa kūkō e ikimasu.

a. 1. (   ) 2. (   ) 3.(   ) 4.(   )

b. 1. (   ) 2. (   ) 3.(   ) 4.(   )

2. Watashi wa itsumo kuruma de machi e ikimasu.

a. 1. (   ) 2. (   ) 3.(   ) 4.(   )

b. 1. (   ) 2. (   ) 3.(   ) 4.(   )

3. Tomodachi wa kinō hikōki de onsen e ikimashita.

a. 1. (   ) 2. (   ) 3.(   ) 4.(   )

b. 1. (   ) 2. (   ) 3.(   ) 4.(   )

4. Hajime ni yama e ikimashō. Sorekara umi e ikimashō.

a. 1. (   ) 2. (   ) 3.(   ) 4.(   )

b. 1. (   ) 2. (   ) 3.(   ) 4.(   )

5. Kinō, Otera e ikimashita ga, oshiro e ikimasen deshita.

a. 1. (   ) 2. (   ) 3.(   ) 4.(   )

b. 1. (   ) 2. (   ) 3.(   ) 4.(   )

Guessing game

1. Anata wa mainichi <u>kaisha</u> e ikimasu ka.
あなたは まいにち <u>かいしゃへ</u> いきますか。

company, town, store, bank, post office, bus stop, friend's house

2. Gakusei wa ashita <u>kaisha</u> e ikimasu ka.
がくせいは あした <u>かいしゃへ</u> いきますか。

company, Tokyo station, hotspring, sea, temple, island, castle

3. Nihonjin wa kinō <u>ginkō</u> e ikimashita ka.
にほんじんは きのう <u>ぎんこう</u>へ いきましたか。

bank, airport, information center, inn, bus stop, friend's school

4. Anata wa itsumo koko e <u>densha</u> de kimasu ka.
あなたは いつも ここへ でんしゃで きますか。

train, bus, plane, ship, bicycle, Bullet Train, on foot

5. Anata wa <u>tenin</u> to issho ni ryōkō shimashita ka.
あなたは てんいんといっしょに りょこうしましたか。

clerk, friend, student, bank worker, Japanese, American, my friend

About myself

1. Watashi wa mainichi aruite koko e kimasu.
2. Kinō watashi wa koko e kuruma de kimashita.
3. Ashita hikoki de Nihon e ikimasu.
4. Kyō kaisha e ikimashita.
5. Itsumo densha de kaerimasu.
6. Watashi no tomodachi wa kinō watashi no ie e kimashita.
7. Watashi wa tomodachi to issho ni Nihon e ryoko shimashita.

Interview

Example questionnaire:

1. Anata wa taitei nani de gakkō e kimasu ka.
2. Kinō anata wa kuruma de machi e ikimashita ka.
3. Anata wa ashita doko e ikimasu ka.
4. Anata wa kyō ie e kaerimasu ka.
5. Nihonjin no tomodachi wa anata no ie e kimashita ka.
6. Tomodachi to issho ni doko e ikimashita ka.
7. Anata wa dare to issho ni ryokō shimashita ka.
8. anata no ie wa doko desu ka.

Constructing a sentence

1. Where is your house?
   どこ、か、あなた、です、いえ、の、は
2. This isn't a Japanese friend's house.
   ありません、ここ、いえ、じゃ、は、にほんじん、の
3. The station is not here.
   ここ、じゃ、えき、ありません、は
4. Over there was the Japanese school.
   あそこ、は、がっこう、の、にほんご、でした
5. Let's go to the town.
   ましょう、まち、いき、へ
6. Shall we go to the tea shop together?
   いっしょに、いき、おちゃ、ましょうか、の、みせ、へ
7. Where shall we go tomorrow?
   どこ、か、いき、あした、ましょう、へ
8. Do you come here every day?
   ここ、きますか、まいにち、へ
9. I go to the mountain on foot.
   あるいて、いきます、へ、やま
10. I returned home by train.
    かえりました、でんしゃ、へ、いえ、で

A letter to your pen pal

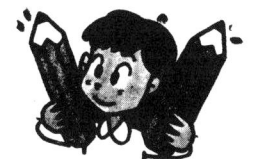

Example:

みちよさん、おげんきですか。
わたしは　げんきです。
これは　わたしの　まちの　ちずです。
まちの　なまえは　スプリングフィールドです。
わたしの　いえは　ここです。
ともだちと　いっしょに　まいにち
スプリングフィールドこうこうへ　バスで　いきます。
みちよさんは　いつも　なにで　がっこうへ
いきますか。
きのう、うみへ　あるいて　いきましたが、
タクシーで　かえりました。
ボブさんと　アンさんと　わたしは　ともだちです。
あした　いっしょに　じてんしゃで　やまへ
いきます。
がっこうへ　いきません。
みちよさんの　ともだちの　なまえは　なんですか。
てがみを　ください。　おげんきで。　　メリーより

Answer the questions about this letter.

1. Mary san wa doko no kōkō e ikimasu ka.
2. Mary san no machi no namae wa nan desu ka.
3. Mary san wa nani de gakkō e ikimasu ka.
4. Kinō umi e nani de ikimashita ka.
5. Mary san no tomodachi no namae wa nan desu ka.

Write a letter to your pen pal.

Evaluation: Listening comprehension

1.
a. I go there today.
b. I don't go there today.
c. I went there today.
d. I didn't go there today.

2.
a. Bob and Ann go.
b. Bob and Ann come.
c. Bob and Ann return.
d. Bob and Ann travel.

3.
a. My house is here.
b. My house is there.
c. My house is over there.
d. My house isn't there.

4.
a. Where is the town?
b. Where is the store?
c. Where is the station?
d. Where is your house?.

5.
a. What?
b. How much?

c. Who?

d. Which one?

6.
a. Let's return there.
b. Shall we return there?
c. I don't return there.
d. I returned there.

7.
a. Let's go together.
b. Let's go slowly.
c. Let's go once more.
d. Let's go now.

8.
a. Did the student come here?
b. Did the bankworker come here?
c. Did the storeclerk come here?
d. Did the friend come here?

9.
a. I traveled but you didn't.
b. I go by train but you go by car.
c. Japanese came but American didn't.
d. I come by bicycle but not on foot.

10.
a. I go to school, then return.
b. The teacher goes to school, then returns.
c. The friend goes to school, then returns.
d. You go to school, then return.

Evaluation: Speaking 1

Page 64

Evaluation: Speaking 2

Scoring guide:	date		name			
a. Vocabulary: variety, new words		0	1	2	3	4
b. Sentence: variety, new structures		0	1	2	3	4
c. Attitude: gesture, eye contact		0	1	2	3	4
d. Voice: clear and natural		0	1	2	3	4
e. Memorized?		0	1	2	3	4

Your total points _____ / 20

Evaluation: Reading and writing

1. Let's go over there tomorrow.
   あした （　　　） へ　いきましょう。

2. Shall we return by train?
   （　　　） で　かえりましょうか。

3. My friends didn't come here.
   わたしの （　　） は （　　　） へ　きませんでした。

4. I travelled with students.
   わたしは （　　　　） といっしょに （　　　　）。

5. Where did you go yesterday?
   きのう　あなたは （　　　） へ （　　　　　）。

6. I went to school, but I didn't go to company.
   （　） へ　いきましたが （　） へいきませんでした。

7. The English teacher and Japanese students didn't come.
   （　） のせんせいと （　　） のがくせいは （　）

8. How will you travel to Japan tomorrow?
   あした　にほん （　） なに （　） りょこうしますか。

Page 65

Lesson 3: Living in Japan

1. You are at a sushi shop with the teacher.

As the teacher tells you what to do, act it out. Later, when you are ready, you can tell other students what to do..

1. Kutsu o nuide kudasai.	Please take off your shoes.
くつを　ぬいで　ください。	
2. Suwatte kudasai.	Please sit down.
すわって　ください。	
3. Nihongo o hanashite kudasai.	Please speak Japanese.
にほんごを　はなして　ください。	
4. Menyu o mite kudasai.	Please look at the men.
メニューを　みて　ください。	
5. Ocha o nonde kudasai.	Please drink tea.
おちゃを　のんで　ください。	
6. Osushi o tabete kudasai.	Please eat sushi.
おすしを　たべて　ください。	

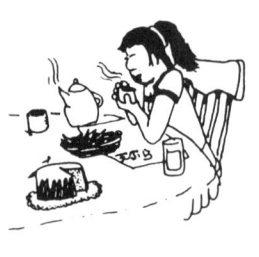
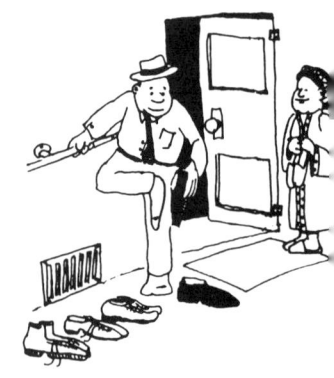

2. Now that you know what to do in a sushiya shop,

even the teacher asks you for advice.

The "te form" follows a complicated, but regular phonetic pattern. If you listen to the tapes often, the correct form of the te form will eventually become automatic.

1. A: Kutsu o nugimashō ka.   Shall I take off my shoes?
   くつを　ぬぎましょうか。
   B Kutsu o nuide kudasai.
   くつを　ぬいで　ください。

2. A: Suwarimashō ka.   Shall I sit down?
   すわりましょうか。
   B: Suwatte kudasai.
   すわって　ください。

3. A: Nihongo o hanashimashō ka.   Shall I speak Japanese?
   にほんごを　はなしましょうか。
   B: Nihongo o hanashite kudasai.
   にほんごを　はなして　ください。

4. A: Menyu o mimashō ka.   Shall I look at the menu?
   メニューを　みましょうか。
   B: Menyu o mite kudasai.
   メニューを　みて　ください。

5. A: Ocha o nomimashō ka.   Shall I drink tea?
   おちゃを　のみましょうか。
   B: Ocha o nonde kudasai.
   おちゃを　のんで　ください。

6. A: Osushi o tabemashō ka.   Shall I eat sushi?
   おすしを　たべましょうか。
   B: Osushi o tabete kudasai.
   おすしを　たべて　ください。

Grammar: (noun) + o + (verb) : direct object

Osushi o tabemashō ka.	Shall we eat sushi?
Jisho o misete kudasai.	Please show me the dictionary.
Nani o mimashita ka.	What did you see?
Okane o kudasai.	Please give me the money.
Ocha o onegai shimasu.	May I have tea?

Grammar: (verb stem) + te kudasai : polite request

		masu form
Kuruma de kaette kudasai.	Please return by car.	*kaerimasu*
Mite kudasai.	Please look.	*mimasu*
Osushi o tabete kudasai.	Please eat the sushi.	*tabemasu*
Nihongo o kaite kudasai.	Please write Japanese.	*kakimasu*
Asoko e itte kudasai.	Please go over there.	*ikimasu*

This is similar to: (noun) + o kudasai.   Please give me the (noun)

Nimotsu o kudasai.	Please give me the luggage.
Kono chizu o kudasai.	Please give me the map.

Grammar: (verb stem) + te

The -te form is used for:
1. -te kudasai : please do -- :   Tabete kudasai.
2. -te imasu : is doing -- :   Tabete imasu.

To make -te form, replace -masu with -te

1. tabe masu ---> tabe te
2. mi masu   ---> mi te
3. ake masu ---> ake te

Phonetic change in the -te form ending:
For many verbs there is a phonetic change in the -te form ending. This depends on
the sound of the last syllable of the verb stem.   Listen to the tapes often, then the
correct form of the te form will eventually become automatic. See Appendix at the back
of the book for a list of -te form verbs.

3. Now you are leaving the sushi shop.

Act it out the teacher's instructions.

1. Tatte kudasai. たって　ください。	Please stand up.
2. Kutsu o haite kudasai. くつを　はいて　ください。	Please put on your shoes.
3. Asoko de okane o haratte kudasai. あそこで　おかねを　はらって　ください。	Please pay the money. over there.
4. To o akete kudasai. とを　あけて　ください。	Please open the door.
5. To o shimete kudasai. とを　しめて　ください。	Please shut the door.
6. S: Machi o aruite kudasai. まちを　あるいて　ください。	Please walk in the town.

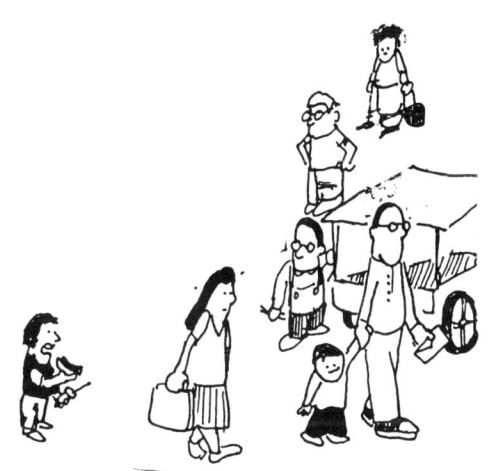

4. It's your turn to ask the teacher to do the same actions.

After doing each action, the teacher will say "I stood up:, etc.

---

1. A: Tatte kudasai.　　　　　　　　Please stand up.
　　 たって　ください。

　 B: Tachimashita.　　　　　　　　 I stood up.
　　 たちました。

2. A: Kutsu o haite kudasai.　　　　Please put on your shoes.
　　 くつを　はいて　ください。

　 B: Hakimashita.　　　　　　　　 I put them on.
　　 はきました。

3. A: Asoko de okane o haratte kudasai.　Please pay money
　　 あそこで　おかねを　はらってください。 over there.

　 B: Haraimashita.　　　　　　　　 I paid it.
　　 はらいました。

4. A: To o akete kudasai.　　　　　 Please open the door.
　　 とを　あけて　ください。

　 B: Akemashita.　　　　　　　　　 I opened it.
　　 あけました。

5. A: To o shimete kudasai.　　　　 Please shut the door.
　　 とを　しめて　ください。

　 B: Shimemashita.　　　　　　　　 I shut it.
　　 しめました。

6. A: Machi o aruite kudasai.　　　 Please walk in the town.
　　 まちを　あるいて　ください。

　 B: Arukimashita.　　　　　　　　 I walked.
　　 あるきました。

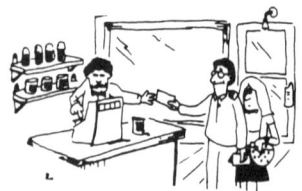

5. Vocabulary : this book,...

kono + noun	kono hon	この ほん	this book
sono + noun	sono hon	その ほん	that book
ano + noun	ano hon	あの ほん	that book over there
dono + noun	dono hon	どの ほん	which book?

6. There are three photographs,

one close to the teacher, one close to you, one far away from both people. The teacher will ask you to show one of the pictures. Answer with; Hai, dozo. (Here it is, please)

Kono shashin o misete kudasai.　Please show me this picture.
この　しゃしんを　みせて　ください。

Substitute: that one over there, that one, this one

7. The teacher would like you to hand her something.

Ano yōhuku o totte kudasai.　Please take those clothes over there.
あの　ようふくを　とって　ください。

Substitute: picture, dictionary, luggage, shoes, tea

8. Someone has left a box on the table, and ...

the teacher wonders whose it is.

A: Kono hako wa dare no desu ka.　　Whose box is this?
この　はこは　だれの　ですか。
B: Bob san no desu.　　It's Bob's.
ボブさんの　です。

Substitute: those clothes over there - Ann, that letter - teacher, these shoes - student , that house - my friend

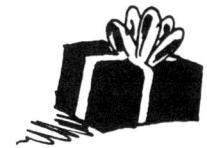

9. The teacher asks Ann where she has gone shopping.

A: <u>Ann san</u> wa dono mise e ikimashita ka. アンさんは　どの　みせへ　いきましたか。	To which store did <u>Ann</u> go?
B: <u>Daimaru</u> e ikimashita. だいまるへ　いきました。	She went to <u>Daimaru</u>.

Substitute: Woolworth's, Sears, The Gap, Kinokuniya, Mitsukoshi

10. And what has Bob been doing?

A: Kinō <u>Bob san</u> wa nani o <u>tabe</u>mashita ka. きのう　ボブさんは　なにを　たべましたか。 <div align="right">What did you <u>eat</u> yesterday, <u>Bob</u>?</div>
B: <u>Tenpura</u> o <u>tabe</u>mashita.　　I ate <u>tempura</u>. てんぷらを　たべました。

Substitute: eat - tempura, drink - tea, look at - T.V., take - picture

11. Vocabulary : Food

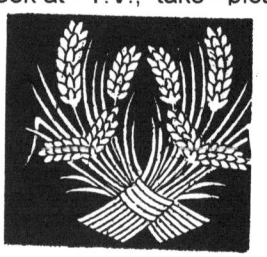

rice, a meal	gohan	ごはん
fish	sakana	さかな
meat	niku	にく
vegetable	yasai	やさい
cakes	okashi	おかし
water	mizu	みず
beer	biiru	ビール
coffee	kōhii	コーヒー
wine	wain	ワイン
milk	miruku	ミルク

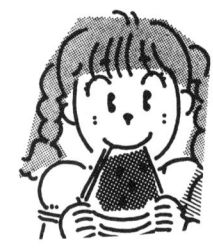

You can figure out how Japanese would pronounce other Western
foods. Use only the sounds from the <u>katakana</u> chart. Every
consonant must be followed by a vowel, except "n". Guess what
these are: "aisukuriimu:, "suteki", "Biggu Makku", "Huraido Poteto".

12. Game

One person thinks of an action, and the other tells where it takes place.

A: Doko de <u>Nihongo o hanashimasu</u> ka. どこで　にほんごを　はなしますか。	Where do you <u>speak Japanese</u>?
B: <u>Resutoran</u> de hanashimasu. レストランで　はなします。	I speak it at <u>a restaurant</u>.

Substitution: take picture - at hotsprings, pay money - at train station,
  drink water - post office, drink Japanese tea - at friend's house

Grammar: (noun) + <u>de</u> + (verb) : location of action

Gakkō de gohan o tabemasu.	I eat a meal at school.
Doko de mizu o nomimashō ka.	Where shall we drink water?
Tegami o koko de yonde kudasai.	Please read the letter here.
Sono mise de okane o haraimashita.	I paid money at the store.

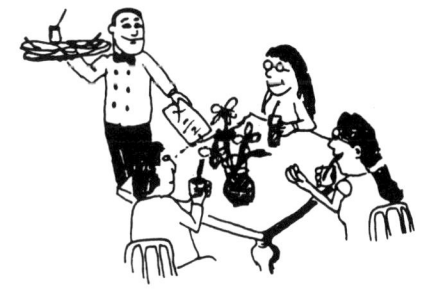

Page 73

13. The teacher is curious about the kind of food Bob is eating.

Ann: Bob san, <u>gohan</u> o tabete kudasai.　Please eat <u>the rice</u>, Bob.
ボブさん、ごはんを　たべて　ください。

Teacher: Bob san, nani o tabete imasu ka. What are you
ボブさんは　なにを　たべて　いますか。 eating, Bob?

Bob: <u>Gohan</u> o tabete imasu.　　　　　I'm eating <u>rice.</u>
ごはんを　たべて　います。

Substitution: fish, meat, vegetable, cake, American cake, this meat

Grammar: (verb stem) + te imasu : progressive action

hanashite imasu　　　　　　　I am speaking.
hanashite imasen　　　　　　　I am not speaking.
hanashite imashita.　　　　　　I was speaking.
hanashiite imasen deshita.　　I was not speaking.
hanashite kudasai.　　　　　　Please speak.

Pattern drill

A: Ima tabete imasu ka.　　　　　　Are you eating now?
いま　たべて　いますか。
B: Tabete imasen.　　　　　　　　I'm not eating.
たべて　いません。
A: Kinō tabete imashita ka.　　　Were you eating yesterday?
きのう　たべて　いましたか。
B: Tabete imasen deshita.　　　　I wasn't eating.
たべて　いません　でした。

Substitute: look, open the book, pay at the station, walk, drink

14. Who is drinking it?

A: Dare ga kōhī o nonde imasu ka.   Who is drinking <u>coffee</u>? だれが　コーヒーを　のんで　いますか。 Bob: <u>Ann san</u> ga nonde imasu   <u>Ann</u> is drinking it. 　　アンさんが　のんで　います。

Substitution: friend, student, Japanese, my teacher, your friend

Grammar: (noun) + ga : emphasize the subject

Use ga to give emphasis to the subject. The question words
(nani, dare, dore, doko) are always used with ga if they are the
subject of the sentence. The answer to such questions also use ga.

Dare ga hanashimasu ka.	**Who** speaks?
Gakusei ga hanashimasu.	**The student** speaks.
Dono tomodachi ga mite imasu ka.	**Which friend** is looking?
Nani ga ii desu ka.	**What** is good?
Doko ga ii desu ka.	**Where** is good?
Dore ga ii desu ka.	**Which** is good?
Sore ga 100 en desu.	**That** is 100 yen.

If you are introducing a general theme without emphasizing it,
<u>wa</u> is used.

A: **Dare** ga okane o haratte imasu ka.	**Who** is paying money?
B: **Sensei** ga haratte imasu.	**The teacher** is paying it.
A: Anata wa?	How about you?
B: Watashi wa **haraimasen**.	I **don't pay**.
Watashi wa tabemasen deshita.	I didn't eat it.
Bob san to Sensei ga tabemashita.	**Bob and the teacher** ate it.

Page 75

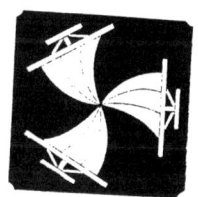

15. Guessing game - what action is the teacher pantomiming?

A: Ima watashi wa nani o shite imasu ka.   What am I doing now?
いま　わたしは　なにを　して　いますか。

B: Aruite imasu.   You're walking.
あるいて　います。

A: Ann san wa aruite imasu ka.   Is Ann walking?
アンさんは　あるいて　いますか。

B: Aruite imasen. Sensei ga aruite imasu. She isn't walking.
あるいて　いません。せんせいが　あるいて　います。
                                   It's the teacher who is walking.

Substitute: pay money, show menu, take shoes off, eat fish

16. Where are you eating a meal?

A: Ima doko de gohan o tabete imasu ka.
いま　どこで　ごはんを　たべていますか。
                          Where are you eating a meal now?
B: Eki de gohan o tabete imasu. I'm eating a meal at the station.
えきで　ごはんを　たべて　います。

Substitute: station, my house, airport, temple, company, bus stop

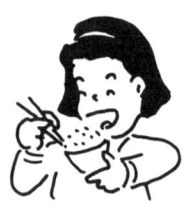

17. Vocabulary: verbs

Verbs: masu form and te form

take off	nugimasu	ぬぎます
		ぬいで
sit down	suwarimasu	すわります
		すわって
speak	hanashimasu	はなします
		はなして
see, look	mimasu	みます
		みて
drink	nomimasu	のみます
		のんで
eat	tabemasu	たべます
		たべて
stand	tachimasu	たちます
		たって
wear (shoes)	hakimasu	はきます
		はいて
pay	haraimasu	はらいます
		はらって
open	akemasu	あけます
		あけて
close	shimemasu	しめます
		しめて
walk	arukimasu	あるきます
		あるいて
show	misemasu	みせます
		みせて
take	torimasu	とります
		とって
sushi shop	sushiya	すしや
shoes	kutsu	くつ
door	to	と
photo	shashin	しゃしん
letter	tegami	てがみ
box	hako	はこ
clothes	yōhuku	ようふく

LET'S PRACTICE SOME MORE.
もっと れんしゅう しましょう。
See Introductory lesson for details.

Vocabulary builders

1. Make cards
2. Listen and stand up

3. Listen and line up
4. Spread on the table

5. Shoots and ladders
6. Around the world

Quick draw + Full house bingo

Expressions

1. Tenin ga kutsu no hako o akete imasu.
2. Amerikajin ga onsen de Nihongo o hanashite imasu.
3. Ginkoin ga otera de okashi o tabete imasu.
4. Tomodachi ga kaisha de ocha o nonde imasu.
5. Sensei ga eki de hon o shimete imasu.
6. Gakusei ga yama de shashin o totte imasu.
7. Nihonjin ga kūkō de nimotsu o misete imasu.
8. Watashi ga mise de yasai to niku o mite imasu.
9. Sensei to gakusei ga umi de kutsu o nuide imasu.

Pattern drill : masu form - te form contrast
1.

A: Tabete kudasai. たべて ください。	Please eat.
B: Tabemasu. Tabemashita. たべます。 たべました。	I will eat. I ate.

2

A: Tabemashō ka. たべましょうか。	Shall we eat?
B: Tabete imasu. たべて います。	I am eating.

Change positive and negative

a. suwarimasu.
b. nomimasen.
c. tachimashita.
d. haraimasen deshita.
e. aruite imasu.
f. tabete imasen.
g. mite imashita.
h. misete imasen deshita.

B's response to A. くみあわせ

A	B
1. Sensei wa ima nani o yonde imasu ka.	Sears
2. Gakusei wa okashi o tabete imasu ka.	tenin
3. Dare ga kutsu o haite imasu ka.	hon
4. Tomodachi wa doko de hanashite imasu ka.	tebete imasen
5. Nihonjin wa dono mise e ikimashita ka.	gakko

Choose from: を、で、で、の、か、と、が、が、へ、は

a. joining two contrasting sentences: (   )
b. by means of, with, using: (   )
c. direct object: (   )
d. theme, as for-: (   )
e. of, modifier, apostrophe-s: (   )
f. to, towards: (   )
g. joining two nouns, and: (   )
h. location of action: (   )
i. question marker: (   )
j emphasize the subject: (   )

Choose one.

1. Who is speaking?
   Dare (ga / de / no) hanashimasu ka.

2. Where did you eat a meal?
   Anata wa doko (o / de / to) gohan o tabemashita ka.

3. I took a photo.
   Watashi wa shashin (e / ka / o) torimashita.

4. The store clerk went to Japan by airplane.
   Tenin wa hikōki (wa / ga / de) Nihon e ikimashita.

5. I took a mountain picture.
   Yama (o / no / e) shashin o torimashtia.

6. The teacher and the student come to school.
   Sensei to gakusei wa gakkō (e / ga / to) kimasu.

7. I eat vegetables but not fish.
   Yasai o tabemasu (o / ga / de), sakana o tabemasen.

8. Please show me this book and that book over there.
   Kono hon (o / ga / to) ano hon o misete kudasai.

9. Where did you pay the money?
   Doko de okane o haraimashita (to / ga / ka)

10. The bankworker spoke.
    Ginkōin (wa / e / no) hanashimashita.

Make verb conjugation list
On the separate sheet, list up <u>masu</u> and <u>te</u> form for each verb.
Organize verbs by same patterns.

Example:

English	masu form	te form
eat	たべます	たべて

1. + て *pattern:*
eat, see, open, close, show, answer, speak, answer, travel, come

2. + って *pattern:*
go, return, sit, stand, take, pay, say, understand

3. *other patterns*
drink, take off, wear (shoes), walk, listen, read, write, wait

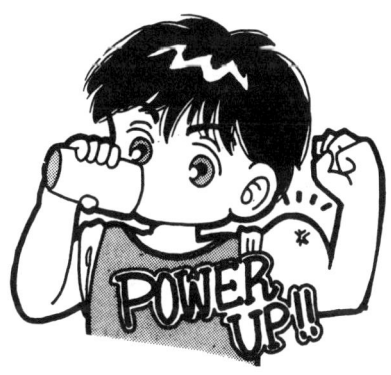

Two way bingo

<u>Basic sentences</u>
Fill in words for substituting.

1. Mainichi watashi wa <u>gakko</u> de <u>shashin</u> o mimasu.

a. 1. (   ) 2. (   ) 3.(   ) 4.(   )

b. 1. (   ) 2. (   ) 3.(   ) 4.(   )

2. Kyo <u>tomodachi</u> wa <u>sakana</u> o tabemasen deshita.

a. 1. (   ) 2. (   ) 3.(   ) 4.(   )

b. 1. (   ) 2. (   ) 3.(   ) 4.(   )

3. Tomodachi ga <u>machi</u> de <u>okashi</u> o tabete imasu.

a. 1. (   ) 2. (   ) 3.(   ) 4.(   )

b. 1. (   ) 2. (   ) 3.(   ) 4.(   )

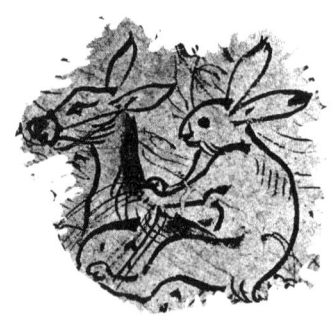

Guessing game

1. Kinō sono gakusei wa <u>sakana</u> o tabemashita ka.
きのう　その　がくせいは　さかなを　たべましたか。

   meat, meal, vegetable, cake, friend's fish, teacher's meat

2. Ano gakusei wa <u>yama</u> o aruite imasu ka.
あの　がくせいは　やまを　あるいて　いますか。

   town, station, airport, island, hotspring, company, temple

3. Ima anata wa <u>oshiro</u> de shashin o totte imasu ka.
いま　おしろで　しゃしんを　とっていますか。

   company, bus stop, information booth, airport, island, station

4. Sono tomodachi wa mainichi <u>aruki</u>masu ka.
その　ともだちは　まいにち　あるきますか。

   take off shoes, look at the mountain, drink Japanese tea, eat rice

5. Kono gakusei wa kinō <u>tabe</u>mashita ka.
この　がくせいは　きのう　たべましたか。

   speak Japanese, put on shoes, open the door, shut the book

6. Ano tenin wa ima <u>suwatte</u> imasu ka.
あの　てんいんは　いま　すわって　いますか。

   speak, walk, stand, open the store, close the door, show

Page 83

About myself

1. ほんを みて います。   Hon o mite imasu.
2. すわって います。   Suwatte imasen.
3. みずを のんで います。   Mizu o nonde imasu.
4. ごはんを たべて います。   Gohan o tabete imasen.
5. あした やまへ いきます。   Ashita yama e ikimasu.
6. きのう いえで しゃしんを とりません でした。
     Kinō ie de shashin o torimasen deshita.
7. まいにち くるまで がっこうへ いきます。
     Mainichi kuruma de gakkō e ikimasu.
8. あした がっこうで にほんごを はなします。
     Ashita gakkō de Nihongo o hanashimasu.
9. きのう ともだちと いっしょに てがみを かきました。
     Kinō tomodachi to issho ni tegami o kakimashita.

Interview

1. あなたは なにを たべますか。   Anata wa nani tabemasu ka.

2. どこで ごはんを たべますか。   Doko de gohan o tabemasu ka.

3. だれが くつを はいて いますか。
     Dare ga kutsu o haite imasu ka.
4. ここで にほんごを はなしますか。
     Koko de Nihongo o hanashimasu ka.
5. いつも どこで おちゃを のみますか。
     Istumo doko de ocha o nomimasu ka.
6. だれが にほんごを はなしますか。
     Dare ga Nihongo o hanashimashita ka.
7. どの レストランで ごはんを たべましたか。
     Dono resutoran de gohan o tabemashita ka.
8. にほんごの せんせいは えいごを はなしますか。
     Nihongo no sensei wa Eigo o hanashimasu ka.
9. だれが やまの しゃしんを とりましたか。
     Dare ga yama no shashin o torimashita ka.

Constructing a sentence

1. Please look at this English dictionary.
   の、じしょ、この、を、みて、えいご、ください

2. I ate a meal at home yesterday.
   で、を、ごはん、きのう、たべ、いえ、ました

3. I didn't drink tea and milk at the store.
   を、ミルク、おちゃ、でした、のみません、と、で、みせ

4. I am speaking Japanese at home.
   はなして、で、いえ、います、にほんご、を

5. What are you doing here?
   か、しています、なに、を、で、ここ

6. Who pays money at school?
   か、はらいます、が、がっこう、を、だれ、おかね、で

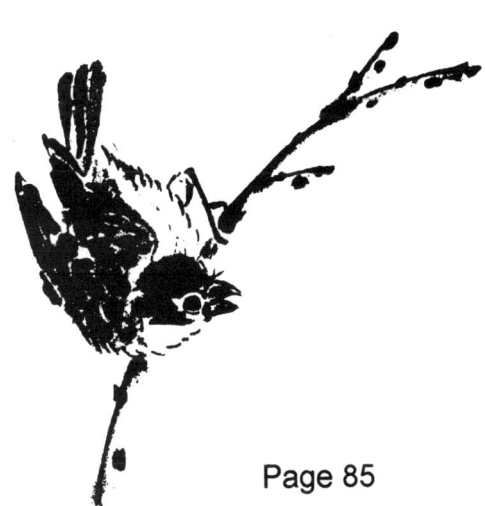

Page 85

A letter to your pen pal

Example:

ひろしさん、おげんきですか。てがみを ありがとう。
きのう にほんの レストランへ いきました。
すしやで おすしを たべました。
にほんの おちゃを のみました。
にほんごを はなしました。
にほんごを よみました。
にほんの テレビを みました。
みせの しゃしんを とりました。
１５ドル はらいました。
この しゃしんを みて ください。

ひろしさんは ハンバーガーを たべますか。
アメリカの みせへ いきましたか。
にほんの レストランの しゃしんを みせて
ください。
にほんの ごはんの しゃしんを みせて ください。
さようなら。 てがみを ください。 おげんきで。
　　　　　　　　ボブより

Answer the question about this letter.

1. Dare ga kono tegami o kakimashita ka.
2. Dare ga Nihon no resutoran e ikimashita ka.
3. Doko de osushi o tabemashita ka.
4. Sushiya de nani o nomimashita ka.
5. Sushiya de nanigo o hanashimashita ka.
6. Bob san wa Nihongo o yomimashita ka, yomimasen deshita ka.
7. Doko no terebi o mimashita ka.
8. Nan no shashin o torimashita ka.
9. Sono mise de ikura haraimashita ka.

Write a letter to your pen pal.

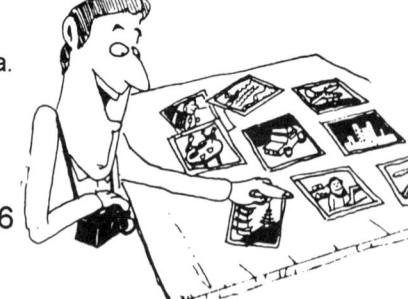

Page 86

Evaluation: Listening comprehension

1.
a. Please close this book.
b. Please open this book.
c. Please look at this book.
d..Please read this book.

6.
a. Where are you paying money?
b. Who is paying money?
c. How much are you paying?
d. What money are you paying?

2.
a. Which letter did he show?
b. Which letter is he showing?
c. Did he show that letter?
d..Is he showing that letter?

7.
a. This clerk ate a meal over there.
b. What did that clerk eat here?
c. Where is that clerk eating a meal?
d. Where did that clerk eat a meal?

3.
a. Where do you drink this?
b. What do you drink here?
c. Which do you drink here?
d..Did you drink this here?

8.
a. Please take pictures here.
b. I am taking pictures here.
c. I am not taking pictures here.
d. Where did you take pictures?

4.
a. Who is walking in town?
b. Who walks in town?
c. Who walked in town?
d..Who was walking in town?

9.
a. Where shall I put these shoes on?
b. I was putting these shoes on at home.
c. I didn't put these shoes on at home.
e. Which shoes shall I put on at home?

5
a. He is always standing.
b. He was always standing.
c. He is not always standing.
d..He was not always standing.

10.
a. Please look at these clothes.
b. Please look at those clothes.
c. Please look at these shoes.
d. Which shoes shall I look at?

Evaluation: Speaking 1

Evaluation: Speaking 2

Scoring guide: date   name

a. Vocabulary: variety, new words	0 1 2 3 4
b. Sentence: variety, new structures	0 1 2 3 4
c. Attitude: gesture, eye contact	0 1 2 3 4
d. Voice: clear and natural	0 1 2 3 4
e. Memorized?	0 1 2 3 4

Your total points   / 20

Evaluation: Reading and writing

1. I eat a meal at school everyday.
   わたしは　まいにち　（　　　）で（　　　）を　たべます。

2. What do you speak at your home?
   あなたの（　　）で　なにを（　　　　　）。

3. Yesterday whose picture did you take in town?
   きのう（　　　）のしゃしんを（　　　）で　とりましたか。

4. Where did you pay money today?
   きょう（　　　）で　おかねを（　　　　　）。

5. Whose watch did you see at the station yesterday?
   きのう（　　　）で　だれの（　　　　）を　みましたか。

6. The teacher drank water and tea at the store.
   せんせい（　）みせ（　）みず（　）おちゃ（　）のみました。

7. In which town is the student walking today?
   きょう　がくせい（　）どの　まち（　）あるいて　いますか。

8. Who took off his shoes at the temple?
   だれ（　）おてら（　）くつ（　）ぬぎましたか。

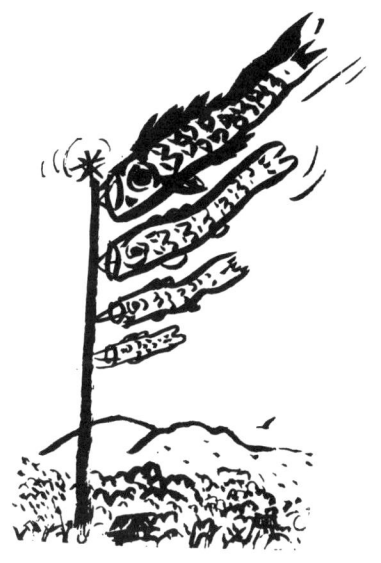

やねより　たかい　こいのぼり

おおきい　まごいは　おとうさん

ちいさい　ひごいは　こどもたち

おもしろそうに　およいでいる

yane yori takai koi nobori	Carp streamers higher than the roof
okii magoi wa otōsan	The big black carp is the father
chiisai higoi wa kodomotachi	The small red carp are the children
omoshiro so ni oyoide iru	They are having fun swimming

1. Let's celebrate Children's Day, *kodomo no hi,* on May 5. Make *koi nobori*, carp streamers, in black, red, blue in various sizes. Put them out in the wind.

2. Make origami helmets. See appendix.
Newspaper is perfect to make helmets to fit your head.

3. Conversation
A: どれが (おとうさん)の こいですか。
   dore ga (otōsan)no koi desu ka. Which is a father carp?
B: あれが (おとうさん)の こいです。
   are ga (otōsan) no koi desu. That is a father carp.

4. Useful expression
(いす)より たかい です。   *(isu)yori takai desu.* I am taller than a chair.

やね yane roof	たかい takai high	こいのぼり koinobori carp streamer	おおきい okii big	おとうさん otōsan father	ちいさい chiisai small	こどもたち kodomotachi children

Lesson 4: Trip to Japan

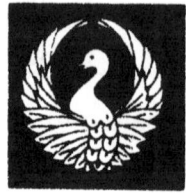

Grammar: (noun) + ni + (verb)

1. Goal of action

Eki ni hairimasu.	I enter the station.
Kutsu o yuka ni okimasu.	I put the shoes on the floor.
Nimotsu ni okashi o iremashita.	I put a cake in the luggage.
Hon ni jusho o kaite kudasai.	Write the address in the book.
Soto ni demasho ka.	Shall we go out?
Kuruma ni notte kudasai.	Please ride in a car.
Okashi o hako ni shimatte kudasai.	Put the cake in the box.
Hako ni okashi o totte kudasai.	Please take the cake in the box.

2. Recipient of action

Tomodachi ni denwa o kakemashō.	Let's call our friends.
Tomodachi ni gakkō de aimashita.	I met friends at school.
Watashi wa tomodachi ni hanashimashita.	I spoke to friends.
Sensei ni tegami o misete kudasai.	Show the letter to the teacher.
Sensei ni namae o itte kudasai.	Please say the name to the teacher
Gakusei wa isu ni suwatte imasu.	Students are sitting on the chairs
Sensei wa gakusei ni hon o agemashita.	Teachers gave books to students.
Tenin ni okane o haraimasen deshita.	I didn't pay money to the clerk.
Nihonjin ni denwa bangō o kikimashō.	Let's ask the phone # to the Japanese person.

3. Location of existence

<u>arimasu</u>: existence of inanimate objects

Hon wa ie ni arimasu.	I have a book at home.
Toire wa koko ni arimasen.	There is no toilet here.
Nimotsu wa eki ni arimashita.	There was luggage at the station.

<u>imasu</u>: existence of animate beings

Gakusei wa doko ni imasu ka.	Where are the students?
Sensei wa gakkō ni imasen deshita.	Teachers weren't at school.
Neko wa watashi no ie ni imasen.	I don't have a cat at home.

1. Action List A: You have arrived in a town in Japan...

where your friend Mori san lives. You go to a phone booth near the station to call Mori san. Practice and demonstrate this skit with your partner.

The -masu form of the verb is given in *Italics*. This can be used to form -masho (let's), -masen (negative), and -mashita (past).

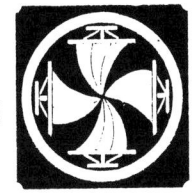

To use the "Action Lists"
First listen and watch as the teacher says each action and acts them out.

Then act them out together with the teacher, as she/he says each action. Later, act them out alone as the teacher speaks.

After enough practice listening to the teacher, you will be able to take the teacher's role and speak while other students act it out.

You can learn quicker and remember more vividly if you actually act it out with real objects.

---

1. Nimotsu o motte imasu.   *mochimasu*
   にもつを　もって　います。I'm holding my luggage.

2. Denwa bokkusu made hakonde imasu.   *hakobimasu*
   でんわ　ボックスまで　はこんで　います。
   I'm carrying it up to the phone booth.

3. Denwa bokkusu ni haitte imasu.   *hairimasu*
   でんわ　ボックスに　はいって　います。
   I'm entering the phone booth.

4. Yuka ni nimotsu o oite imasu.   *okimasu*
   ゆかに　にもつを　おいて　います。
   I'm putting the luggage on the floor.

5. Denwa no kakekata o yonde imasu.   *yomimasu*
   でんわの　かけかたを　よんで　います。
   I'm reading "How to make a phone call".

Page 91

2. The teacher is offering to help carry your luggage.

1.

A: にもつを　もちましょうか。　　　　Nimotsu o mochimashō ka.

B: もって　ください。　　　　　　　　Motte kudasai.

2.

A: でんわボックスまで　はこびましょうか。
　　　　　　　　　　　　　Denwa bokkusu made hakobimashō ka.

B: はこんで　ください。　Hakonde kudasai.

3.

A: でんわボックスに　はいりましょうか。
　　　　　　　　　　　　　Denwa bokkusu ni hairimashō ka.

B: はいって　ください。　Haitte kudasai.

4.

A: ゆかに　にもつを　おきましょうか。
　　　　　　　　　　　　　Yuka ni nimotsu o okimashō ka.

B: おいて　ください。　Oite kudasai.

5.

A: でんわの　かけかたを　よみましょうか。
　　　　　　　　　　　　　Denwa no kakekata o yomimashō ka.

B: よんで　ください。　Yonde kudasai.

Answer about the skit.

1. なにを　もって　いますか。　　　　Nani o motte imashita ka.

2. どこまで　にもつを　はこびましたか。
　　　　　　　　　　　　Doko made nimotsu o hakobimashita ka.

3. どこに　はいりましたか。　　　　Doko ni hairimashita ka.

4. どこに　にもつを　おきましたか。
　　　　　　　　　　　　Doko ni nimotsu o okimashita ka.

5. なにを　よみましたか。　　　　　Nani o yomimashita ka.

3. Action List B: Telephoning Mori san

6. Poketto kara jū en o dashite imasu.   *dashimasu*
ポケットから　１０えんを　だして　います。
> I'm taking out 10 yen from my pocket.

7. Denwa ni jū en o irete imasu.   *iremasu*
でんわに　１０えんを　いれて　います。
> I'm putting the 10 yen into the phone.

8. Mori san ni denwa o kakete imasu.   *kakemasu*
もりさんに　でんわを　かけて　います。
> I'm telephoning Mori san.

9. Kami ni jūsho o kaiite imasu.   *kakimasu*
かみに　じゅしょを　かいて　います。
> I'm writing the address on paper.

10. Soto ni dete imasu.   *demasu*
そとに　でて　います。
> I'm going outside..

4. The teacher is offering to help make the phone call.

6.
A: ポケットから　じゅうえんを　だしましょうか。
　　Poketto kara jū en o dashimashō ka.
B: だして　ください。　Dashite kudasai.

7.
A: でんわに　じゅうえんを　いれましょうか。
　　Denwa ni jū en o iremashō ka.
B: いれて　ください。　Irete kudasai.

8.
A: もりさんに　でhわを　かけましょうか。
　　Mori san ni denwa o kakemashō ka.
B: かけて　ください。　Kakete kudasai.

10.
A: そとに　でましょうか。Soto ni demashō ka.

B: でて　ください。　Dete kudasai.

Answer about the skit.

1. どこから　じゅうえんを　だしましたか。
   Doko kara jū en o dashimashita ka.
2. どこに　じゅうえんを　いれましたか。
   Doko ni jū en o iremashita ka.
3. だれに　でんわを　かけましたか。
   Dare ni denwa o kakemashita ka.
4. なにに　じゅうしょを　かきましたか。
   Nani ni jūsho o kakimashita ka.
5. そとに　でましたか。　Soto ni demashita ka.

5. Action List C: Taking the bus to Mori's house

11. Mise de omiyage o katte imasu.　　　　　　*kaimasu*
    みせで　おみやげを　かって　います。
    I'm buying a souvenir gift at a store..
12. Tenin ni basu noriba o kiite imasu.　　　　*kikimasu*
    てんいんに　バスのりばを　きいて　います。
    I'm asking the store clerk about the bus stop.
13. Basu noriba de basu o matte imasu.　　　　*machimas*
    バスのりばで　バスを　まって　います。
    I'm waiting for the bus at the bus stop.
14. Basu ni notte imasu.　　　　　　　　　　*norimasu*
    バスに　のって　います。
    I'm getting on the bus.
15. Untenshu ni Mori san no jūsho o itte imasu.　*iimasu*
    うんてんしゅに　もりさんのじゅうしょを　いって　います。
    I'm saying Mori san's address to the driver.
16. Yūbinkyoku de basu o orite imasu.　　　　*orimasu*
    ゆうびんきょくで　バスを　おりて　います。
    I'm getting off the bus at the post office.

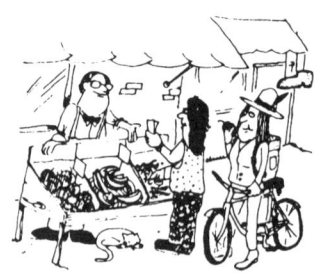
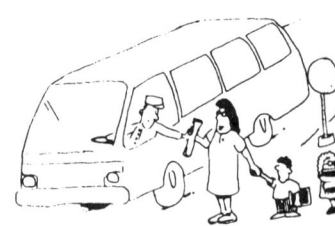

6. The teacher is offering to help with the vist
and the bus ride.

11. A: みせで おみやげを かいましょうか。
　　　　　　　　　　　　Mise de omiyage o kaimashō ka.
　　B: かって ください。　Katte kudasai.

12. A: てんいんに バスのりばを ききましょうか。
　　　　　　　　　　　　Tenin ni basu noriba o kikimashō ka.
　　B: きいて ください。　　　Kiite kudasai.

13. A: バスのりばで バスを まちましょうか。
　　　　　　　　　　　　Basu noriba de basu o machimashō ka.
　　B: まって ください。　　　Matte kudasai.

14. A: バスに のりましょうか。　　Basu ni norimashō ka.

　　B: のって ください。　　　　Notte kudasai.

15. A: うんてんしゅに もりさんのじゅうしょをいいましょうか。
　　　　　　　　　　Untenshu ni Mori san no jūsho o iimashō ka.
　　B: いって ください。　Itte kudasai.

16. A: ゆうびんんきょくで バスを おりましょうか。
　　　　　　　　　　　Yūbinkyoku de basu o orimashō ka.
　　B: おりて ください。　Orite kudasai.

Answer about the skit.

1. どこで おみやげを かいましたか。
   Doko de omiyage o kaimashita ka.
2. だれに バスのりばを ききましたか。
   Dare ni basu noriba o kikimashita ka.
3. どこで バスを まちましたか。
   Doko de basu o machimashita ka.
4. だれに もりさんの じゅうしょを いいましたか。
   Dare ni Mori san no jūsho o iimashita ka.
5. どこで バスを おりましたか。　Doko de basu o orimashita ka.

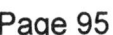

Page 95

7. Action List D: Visiting with Mori san

17. Mori san ni yūbinkyoku de atte imasu.   *aimasu*
    もりさんに　ゆうびんきょくで　あって　います。
    I'm meeting Mori san at the post office.
18. Mori san no ie de isu ni suwatte imasu.   *suwarimasu*
    もりさんの　いえで　いすに　すわって　います。
    I'm sitting in a chair in Mori san's house.
19. Mori san ni omiyage o agete imasu.   *agemasu*
    もりさんに　おみやげを　あげて　います。
    I'm giving a souvenir gift to Mori san.
20. Mori san kara omiyage o moratte imasu   *moraimasu*
    もりさんから　おみやげを　もらって　います。
    I'm receiving a souvenir gift from Mori san.
21. Nimotsu ni omiyage o shimatte imasu.   *shimaimasu*
    にもつに　おみやげを　しまって　います。
    I'm putting the gift away in my luggage.

8. The teacher offers to help with the visit.

17.A: もりさんに　ゆうびんきょくで　あいましょうか。
    Mori san ni yūbinkyoku de aimashō ka.
    B: あって　ください。   Atte kudasai.

18.A: もりさんの　いえで　いすに　すわりましょうか。
    Mori san no ie de isu ni suwarimashō ka.
    B: すわって　ください。   Suwatte kudasai.

19.A: もりさんに　おみやげを　あげましょうか。
    Mori san ni omiyage o agemashō ka.
    B: あげて　ください。   Agete kudasai.

20.A: もりさんから　おみやげを　もらいましょうか。
    Mori san kara omiyage o moraimashō ka.
    B: もらって　ください。   Moratte kudasai.

21.A: にもつに　おみやげを　しまいましょうか。
    Nimotsu ni omiyage o shimaimashō ka.
    B: しまって　ください。   Shimatte kudasai.

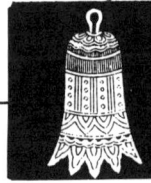

Answer about the skit.

1. だれに　ゆうびんきょくで　あいましたか。
   Dare ni yūbinkyoku de aimashita ka.
2. もりさんの　いえで　なにに　すわりましたか。
   Mori san no ie de nani ni suwarimashita ka.
3. だれに　おみやげを　あげましたか。
   Dare ni omiyage o agemashita ka.
4. だれから　おみやげを　もらいましたか。
   Dare kara omiyage o moraimashita ka.
5. どこに　おみやげを　しまいましたか。
   Doko ni omiyage o shimaimashita ka.

9. Create your own actions
by combining verbs you have learned with other vocabulary.

A: かみに　じゅうしょを　かいて　ください。
   Kami ni jūsho o kaite kudasai.
                          Please write the address on the paper.
B: かきました。
   Kakimashita.   I wrote it.

Substitute:
1. write address on paper
2. put pen into pocket
3. put books in luggage
4. go outside
5. enter the room
6. sit down in chair
7. put pen on table

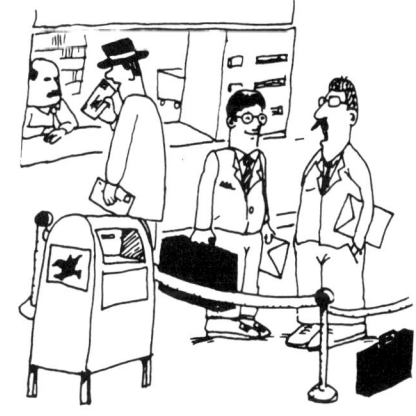

10. Use the particle "ni" to tell who received the action.

A: だれに　あいましたか。
Dare ni <u>aimashita</u> ka.　　　　　Whom did you <u>meet</u>?
B: ともだちに　あいました。
<u>Tomodachi</u> ni <u>aimashita</u>.　　　I met a friend.

Substitute:
1. meet - friend
2. speak Japanese - to teacher
3. tell name - to bank worker
4. ask telephone number - to store clerk
5. show photo - to student
6. give photo - to friend
7. pay money - to driver
8. telephone - to Japanese friend
9. write letter - to teacher's friend

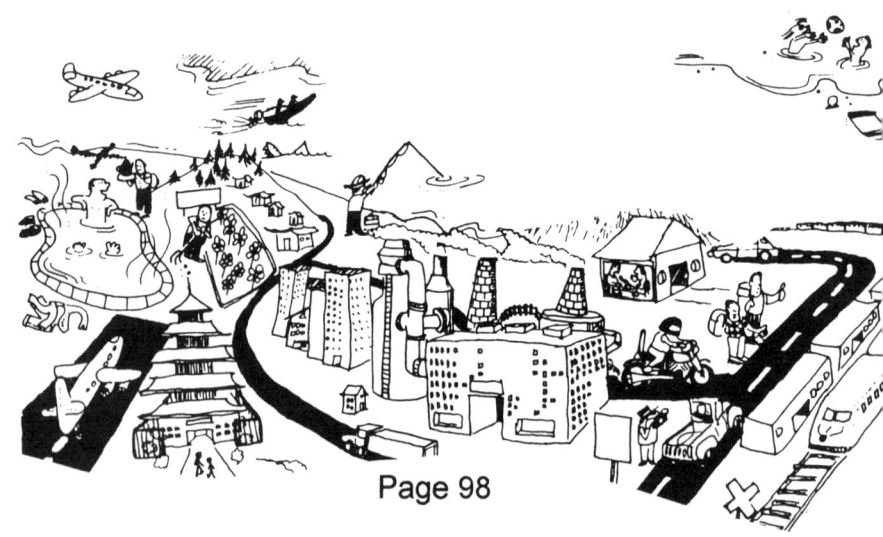

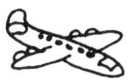

11. A report from Bob (part 1)   Bob's arrival in Japan

1. Narita kūkō ni tsukimashita.   I arrived at Narita Airport.
なりた　くうこうに　つきました。   ついて

2. Hikōki wa okuremashita.   The airplane was late.
ひこうきは　おくれました。   おくれて

3. Watashi wa tsukaremashita.   I was tired.
わたしは　つかれました。   つかれて

4. Ame ga hutte imashita.   It was raining.
あめが　ふって　いました。   ふります

5. Tōkyō no ryokan ni tomarimashita. I stayed at an inn in Tokyo.
とうきょうの　りょかんに　とまりました。   とまって

12. Ask each other about Bob's arrival in Japan.

1 ・ Dono kūkō ni tsukimashita ka.
どの　くうこうに　つきましたか。

2 ・ Hikōki wa okuremashita ka.
ひこうきは　おくれましたか。

3 ・ Bob san wa tsukaremashita ka, tsukaremasen deshita ka.
ボブさんは　つかれましたか、つかれません　でしたか。

4 ・ Ame ga hutte imashita ka.
あめが　ふって　いましたか。

5 ・ Doko ni tomarimashita ka.
どこに　とまりましたか。

13. Ask each other similar questions about each other.

1. Is it raining now?
2. Are you going to stay at a friend's house today?
3. Were you tired yesterday?
4. Were you late?

14. A report from Bob (part 2)   Living in Kyoto

6. Ima Kyōto ni sunde imasu.   I live in Kyoto now.
   いま　きょうとに　すんで　います。

7. Watashi no ie kara otera ga miemasu.   A temple is visible
   わたしの　いえから　おてらが　みえます。   from my house.

8. Watashi wa Nihongo ga dekimasen.   I can't speak Japanese.
   わたしは　にほんごが　できません。

9. Kyōto no gakkō de Nihongo o benkyō shite imasu.
   きょうとのがっこうで　にほんごを　べんきょう　しています。
                          I'm studying Japanese at a school in Kyoto.

15. Ask each other questions about Bob's report.

1. Ima dono machi ni sunde imasu ka.
   いま　どの　まちに　すんで　いますか。

2. Bob san no ie kara nani ga miemasu ka.
   ボブさんの　いえから　なにが　みえますか。

3. Bob san wa Nihongo ga dekimasu ka.
   ボブさんは　にほんごが　できますか。

4. Doko no gakkō de Nihongo o benkyō shite imasu ka.
   どこの　がっこうで　にほんごを　べんきょうして　いますか。

16. Ask each other questions similar to 4-14 about each other.

1. Where do you live?
2. What can be seen from school?
3. Can you play golf?
4. What are you studying?

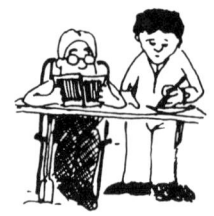

17. A report from Bob (part 3) teaching English in Japan

10. Mainichi Eigo o oshiete imasu.　　I teach English every day.
    まいにち　えいごを　おしえて　います。

11. Hachi ji kara yo ji made hatarakimasu. I work from 8 to 4.
    8じから　4じまで　はたらきます。

12. Kyō tomodachi ga ie ni kimasu.　　Today, friends will come
    きょう　ともだちが　いえに　きます。　　to my home.

13. Watashi wa kimono o kimasu.　　I'll wear a kimono.
    わたしは　きものを　きます。

14. Sukiyaki o tsukurimasu.　　I'll make sukiyoaki.
    すきやきを　つくります。

18. Ask each other about the last part of Bob's report.

1. Mainichi nani o oshiete imasu ka.
   まいにち　なにを　おしえて　いますか。

2. Nan ji kara nanji made hatarakimasu ka.
   なんじから　なんじまで　はたらきますか。

3. Kyō dare ga ie ni kimasu ka.
   きょう　だれが　いえに　きましたか。

4. Bob san wa nani o kimasu ka.
   ボブさんは　なにを　きましたか。

5. Nani o tsukurimasu ka.
   なにを　つくりましたか。

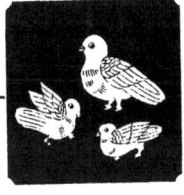

19. Ask each other similar questions about each other.

1. Who is teaching Japanese here?
2. From what time to what time do you study?
3. Who came to your school?
4. What are you wearing now?
5. What did you make yesterday?

20. Pattern drill: --te imasu

A: Ann san wa benkyō shite imasu ka. Is Ann studying?
　アンさんは　べんきょうして　いますか。

B: <u>Shi</u>te imasen.   She is not studying.
　して　いません。

A: Kinō <u>shi</u>te imashita ka.   Was she studying yesterday?
　きのう　して　いましたか。

B: <u>Shi</u>te imasen deshita.   She was not studying.
　して　いません　でした。

Substitute: study, work, wear kimono, make sushi, have money, carry luggage, read newspaper, write a letter, listen to radio

21. My daily life

Make your own report similar to Bob's, telling of your own daily life. Ask the teacher to help you with sentences you are not sure of.

Share your report in class, so other students can ask you questions about it.

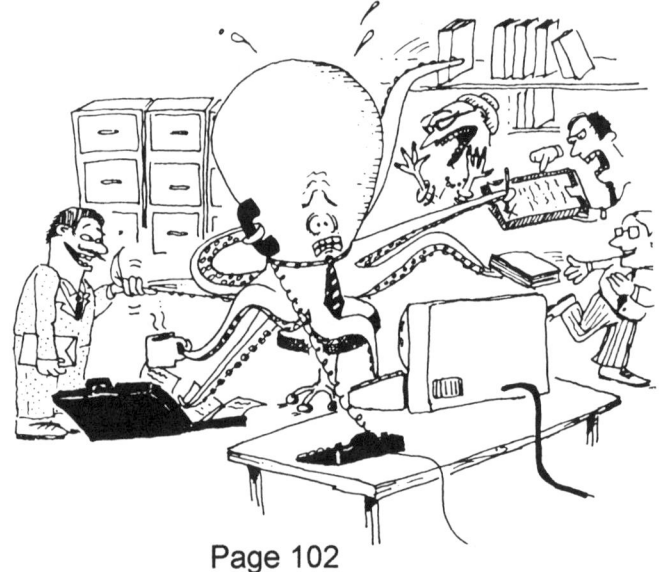

Page 102

Grammar: arimasu, imasu, desu : to be

Japanese has three kinds of "to be" verbs:

1. arimasu: existence of inanimate objects

Terebi wa arimasen.	There is no T.V.
Nani ga koko ni arimasu ka.	What is at the school?
Kuruma wa asoko ni arimashita.	The car is located over there
Okane wa ie ni arimasen deshita.	Themoney was not at home.
Tokyo iki no kippu wa arimasu ka.	Do you have a ticket to Tokyo?

2. imasu: existence of people, animate beings, cats,...

Sensei wa koko ni imasu ka.	Is there a teacher here?
Dare ga asoko ni imashita ka.	Who was over there?
Gakusei wa doko ni imasu ka.	Where is the students?
Watashi no neko wa koko ni imasen.	My cat is not here.
Konō neko wa heya ni imashita.	This cat was in the room.

3. a. (noun A) wa (noun B) desu : (noun A) = (noun B)
   b. (noun A) wa (adjective C) desu :

   (noun A) is described by adjective C)

Bob san wa Amerikajin desu.	Bob is an American.
Kore wa ocha desu.	This is tea.
Ann san wa nan desu ka.	Which one is Ann?
Kippu wa ikura desu ka.	How much is the ticket?
Nihongo no sensei wa dare desu ka.	Which is Japanese teacher?

Bob san wa omoshiroi desu.	Bob is interesting.
Kore wa oishii desu.	This is delicious.

(Adjectives will be studied in Lesson 5.)

Desu is sometimes used for ni arimasu, ni imasu.

Jisho wa koko ni arimasu. = Jisho wa koko desu.
Gakusei wa doko ni imasu ka.= gakusei wa doko desu ka.
Watashi no nimotsu wa eki ni arimashita.
             = Watashi no nimotsu wa eki deshita.

22. The teacher is looking for a mailbox.

A: <u>Posto</u> wa arimasu ka. ポストは　ありますか。	Is there <u>a mailbox</u>?
B: Arimasu. あります。	There is.
A: Doko ni arimasu ka. どこに　ありますか。	Where is it?
B: <u>Asoko</u> ni arimasu. あそこに　あります。	It's <u>over there</u>.

Substitute:　Bob's letter, stamps, Japanese money, bank, store

23. What do you have there?

A: Nani ga soko ni arimasu ka. なにが　そこに　ありますか。	What do you have there?
B: <u>Ann san no tegami</u> ga arimasu. アンさんの　てがみが　あります。	There is <u>Ann's letter.</u>
A: <u>Shashin</u> mo arimasu ka. しゃしんも　ありますか。	Are there <u>pictures</u>, too?
B: Arimasen. ありません。	There aren't.

Substitute:　clothes - kimono,　book - dictionary,　ticket - money

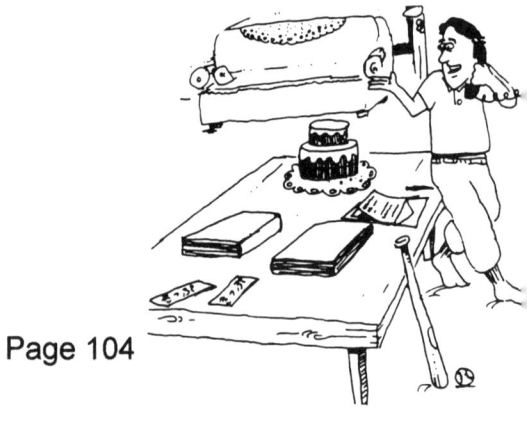

Grammar: mo : also, too

1. Mo can replace wa, o, ga.

Watashi wa gakusei desu.	I am a student.
Bob san mo gakusei desu.	Bob is a student, too.
Nihongo o benkyō shimasu.	I study Japanese.
Eigo mo benkyō shimasu.	I study English, too.
Hon ga gakkō ni arimasu.	There is a book at school.
Kami mo arimasu.	There is paper, too.

2. Adding mo to other particles: e, de, ni, kara, made, to: also.

Tokyo e ikimasu. Kyoto emo ikimasu.
Densha de yama e ikimasu. Jitensha demo ikimasu.
Gakkō de Nihongo o hanashimasu. Ie demo hanashimasu.
Bob san ni aimashita. Ann san nimo aimashita.
Koko ni okashi ga arimasu. Asoko nimo arimasu.
Tegami ga Nihon kara kimashita. Amerika kara mo kimashita.
Gakusei to hanashimasu, Sensei tomo hanashimasu.

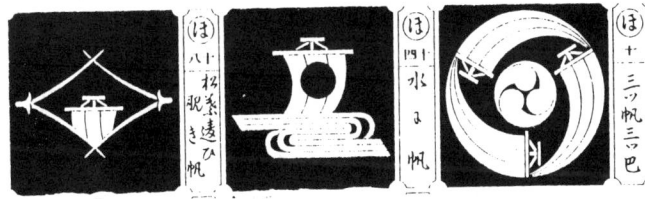

Ask each other where various things are.

A: <u>okane</u> wa doko ni arimasu ka. おかねは　どこに　ありますか。	Where is <u>the money</u>?
B: <u>Poketto</u> ni arimasu. ポケットに　あります。	It's in <u>the pocket</u>.

Substite: ticket - luggage, watch - here, car - over there

24. The teacher is telephoning Ann's house, but Ann isn't there.

A: Moshi moshi, <u>Ann san</u> wa imasu ka. もしもし、アンさんは　いますか。	Hello; is <u>Ann</u> there?
B: Imasen. いません。	She's not.
A: <u>Ann san</u> wa doko ni imasu ka. アンさんは　どこに　いますか。	Where is <u>Ann</u>?
B: <u>Nihon</u> ni imasu. にほんに　います。	She's in <u>Japan</u>.

Substitute: Michiyo - restaurant, Bob - company, friend - store

Ask where the people in the class are.

A: <u>Sensei</u> wa doko ni imasu ka. せんせいは　どこに　いますか。
B: <u>Asoko</u> ni imasu. あそこに　います。

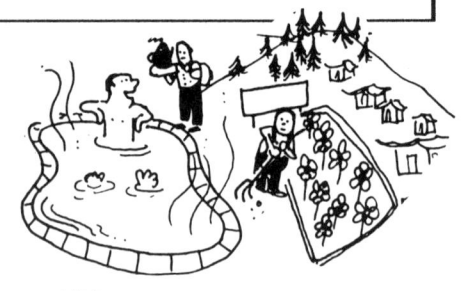

25. The teacher notices that you need something.

A: Nani ga irimasu ka.	What do you need?
なにが　いりますか。	
B: <u>Nihongo no jisho</u> ga irimasu.	I need a <u>Japanese dictionary</u>.
にほんごの　じしょが　いります。	
A: <u>Eigo</u> no wa?	How about an <u>English one</u>?
えいごのは。	
B: <u>Eigo</u> no wa irimasen.	I don't need one.
えいごのは　いりません。	

Substitute: American money - Japanese one,
 ticket to Kyoto - one to Tokyo, mountain map - town map

Ask other students what they need to take with them on their trip

A: Nani ga irimasu ka.
　　なにが　いりますか。
B: <u>Kippu</u> ga irimasu.
　　きっぷが　いります。

26. Vocabulary

floor	yuka	ゆか
the way to call	kakekata	かけかた
address	jūsho	じゅうしょ
outside	soto	そと
souvenir gift	omiyage	おみやげ
driver	untenshu	うんてんしゅ
chair	isu	いす
mailbox	posuto	ポスト
rain	ame	あめ
study	benkyō	べんきょう
kimono	kimono	きもの
photo	shashin	しゃしん
stamp	kitte	きって
room	heya	へや
hello for call	moshimoshi	もしもし
cat	neko	ねこ

LET'S PRACTICE SOME MORE.
もっと れんしゅう しましょう。
See Introductory lesson for details.

Vocabulary builders

1. **Make cards**

2. **Listen and stand up**

3. **Listen and line up**

4. **Spread on the table**

5. **Shoots and ladders**

6. **Around the world**

Quick draw + Full house bingo

Expressions

1. Sensei wa hako ni haitte imasu.
2. Ginkōin wa sakana o isu ni oite imasu.
3. Nimotsu kara tokei o dashite imasu.
4. Heya ni isu o irete imasu.
5. Yuka ni namae o kaite imasu.
6. Hikōki ni notte imasu.
7. Gakusei ni otera de atte imasu.
8. Tenin ni jisho o agete imasu.
9. Kuruma ni yōhuku o shimatte imasu.
10. Watashi wa yama ni sunde imasu.

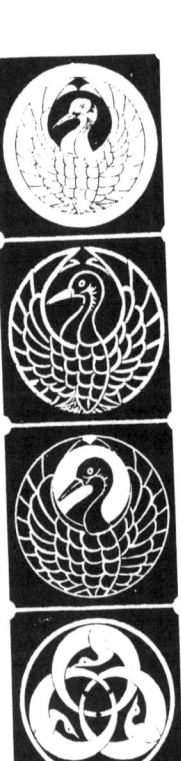

Make verb conjugation list.

On a separate sheet, list masu and te forms for each verb.
Organize verbs by same patterns.

Example:

English	masu form	te form
eat	たべます	たべて

+ て pattern:

take out, put in, phone, go out, get down, give, be late, be tired

be visible, can do, study, teach, wear, there is (animate)

open, come, do, speak, can see, show, close, eat, answer

+ って pattern:

hold, enter, buy, wait, ride, say, meet, sit down, receive

put away, rain, make, there is (inanimate), need, pay, go

return, wait, stand, stop/stay, take, understand

other patterns:

-nde: carry, read, live, drink

-ite: put down, write, ask, arrive, work, walk, put on foot, hear

-ide: take off

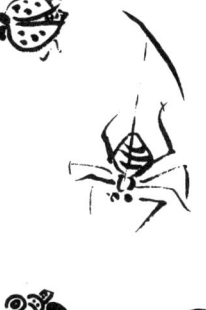

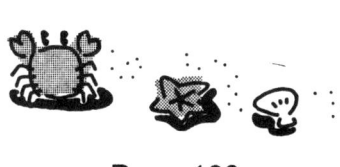

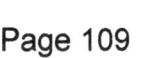

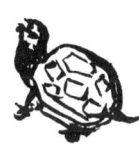

Particle: Fill in ( ).
Choose from:
を、まで、で、で、に、の、か、と、も、が、が、から、へ、は

a. also, too: (   )
b. until: (   )
c. joining two contrasting sentences: (   )
d. by means of, with, using: (   )
e. direct object: (   )
f. goal of action, recipient of action, location of existence: (   )
g. from: (   )
h. theme, as for-: (   )
i. of, modifier, apostrophe-s: (   )
j. to, towards: (   )
k. joining two nouns, and: (   )
l. location of action: (   )
m. question marker: (   )
n. emphasize the subject: (   )

Choose one.

1. Sensei wa dare (ga / ni / no) hanashimasu ka.
2. Anata wa doko (o / de / ni) kuruma o okimashita ka.
3. Yama o arukimashita. Shashin (e / ka / mo) torimashita.
4. Hikōki (wa / kara / de) orite kudasai.
5. Ano yama (ga / no /made) arukimashō.
6. Sensei to gakusei wa watashi no ie (e / ga / to) aruite kimashita.
7. Machi de yasai o kaimasu (o / ga / de), sakana o kaimasen.
8. Kono okashi (o / ga / to) ano yasai o tomodachi ni agemashō.
9. Dare ni okane o haraimashita (to / ga / ka)
10. Untenshu (wa / e / no) watashi ni hanashimashita.

Two way bingo

Basic sentences
1. <u>Gakusei</u> wa <u>hon</u> ga irimasu.

a. 1. (   ) 2. (   ) 3.(   ) 4.(   )
b. 1. (   ) 2. (   ) 3.(   ) 4.(   )

2. Sono <u>untenshu</u> wa <u>Nihongo</u> ga dekimasu.

a. 1. (   ) 2. (   ) 3.(   ) 4.(   )
b. 1. (   ) 2. (   ) 3.(   ) 4.(   )

3. Sensei no <u>nimotsu</u> wa <u>kuruma</u> ni arimasu.

a. 1. (   ) 2. (   ) 3.(   ) 4.(   )
b. 1. (   ) 2. (   ) 3.(   ) 4.(   )

Guessing game
1. Anata no tomodachi wa <u>kaishain</u> ni aimashita ka.
あなたの　ともだちは　かいしゃいんに　あいましたか。

company worker, clerk, Japanese student, teacher, driver,

2. Anata wa <u>densha</u> ni norimashita ka.
あなたは　でんしゃに　のりましたか。

train, taxi, Bullet Train, Japanese airplane, boat, Japanese train

3. Eigo no sensei wa <u>gakusei</u> ni denwa o kakemashita ka.
えいごの　せんせいは　がくせいに　でんわを　かけましたか。

students, driver, Japanese, clerk, company worker, my friend

4. Ginkō in wa <u>8ji</u> kara hatarakimasu ka.
ぎんこういんは　8じから　はたらきますか。

8 o'clock, 9 o'clock, 10 o'clock, 11 o'clock, 12 o'clock

About myself

1. Watashi wa kinō sensei ni hana o agemashita.
2. Tomodachi kara kuruma o moraimashita.
3, Mainichi tomodachi ni denwa o kakemasu.
4. Kinō Nihonjin ni aimashita.
5. Watashi no ie ni Nihon no kuruma ga arimasu.
6. Kono gakkō ni Nihonjin wa imasen.
7. Kyō Nihongo de tegami o pen pal ni kakimashita.
8. Watashi wa ima machi ni sunde imasu.
9. Itsumo enpitsu o nimotsu ni iremasu.
10. Okane o watashi no poketto ni shimaimasu.

Interview

Examples:

1. Ima anata no ie ni Nihon no okane ga arimasu ka.
2. Ima anata no gakkō ni Nihonjin ga imasu ka.
3. Gakkō de nani ga irimasu ka.
4. Piano ga dekimasu ka.
5. Anata no gakkō no denwa bangō ga wakarimasu ka.
6. Koko kara nani ga miemasu ka.
7. Mainichi kuruma ni norimasu ka.
8. Dare ni tegami o kakimashita ka.
9. Nihongo no jisho o motte imasu ka.
10. Doko ni sunde imasu ka.

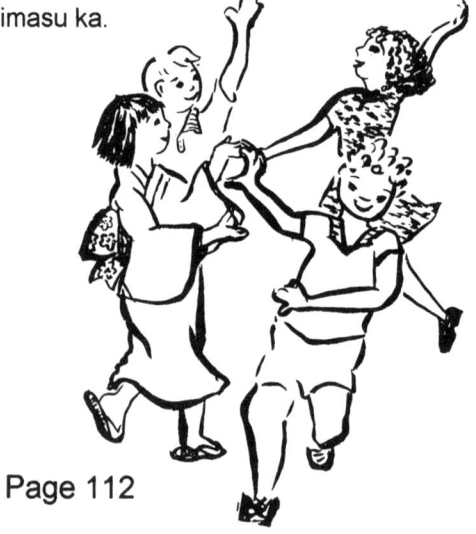

Constructing a sentence

1, I entered the store.
わたし、に、は、みせ、はいりました

2, Please carry the box up to the car.
ください、くるま、はこんで、を、まで、はこ

3. Please take the chair away from the room.
ください、だして、を、から、へや、いす

4. I wrote my name on the paper with a pen at school
なまえ、を、の、わたし、かきました、がっこう、
で、かみ、に、ペン、

5. I met a friend at the company.
あいました、に、で、かいしゃ、ともだち

6. Please give the flower to your friend.
の、ともだち、あげて、はな、ください、
を、あなた、に

7. I received a book from my teacher.
もらい、ほん、ました、を、せんせい、
わたし、から、の

8. I live in Tokyo now.
いま、に、すんで、とうきょう、います

9. I work from 9 to 5.
から、まで、ごじ、くじ、はたらきます

10, I have money in my luggage.
おかね、あります、わたし、にもつ、の、に

11. Do you have a friend at school?
か、に、がっこう、ともだち、います

A letter to your pen pal

こんにちは、ボブさん。おげんきですか。
わたしは　とても　げんきです。
ボブさんは　まいにち　なにを　しますか。
わたしは　オレンジジュースを　のみます。
トーストを　たべます。シャワーに　はいります。
せいふくを　きます。かばんに　ほんを　いれます。
それから　まいにち　がっこうへ　あるいていきます。
ときどき　あめが　ふりますが　バスに　のりません。
がっこうに　おくれません。
がっこうは　わたしの　まちに　あります。
わたしは　ともだちに　にほんごを　おしえます。
にほんじんの　がくせいと　にほんごを　はなします。
にほんごの　クラスで　えいがを　みます。
にほんごの　しんぶんを　よみます。
にほんごの　テープを　ききます。
そとで　テニスを　します。
にほんの　おかしを　つくります。
がっこうの　そとで　しゃしんを　とります。
えいごの　べんきょうを　します。
とても　つかれます。
それから　いえに　かえります。
ときどき　ともだちに　でんわを　かけます。
わたしの　いえに　いぬと　ねこが　います。
わたしの　へやに　コンピューターが　あります。
わたしの　へやで　べんきょうを　します。
それから　ねます。　おやすみなさい。　　ひろしより

Answer the questions about the letter.

１、ひろしさんは　なにを　のみますか。
２、せいふくを　きますか、きませんか。
３、くるまで　がっこうへ　いきますか。
４、がっこうは　どこに　ありますか。
５、ひろしさんは　だれに　にほんごを　おしえますか。

Write a letter to a pen pal.

Page 114

Evaluation: Listening comprehension

1.
a. Where is the flower?
b. The flower is over there.
c. Whose flower is over there?
d. Do you need a flower?

6.
a. What can you see from here?
b. Is the sea visible from here?
c. From where is the sea visible?
d. The sea is also visible from here.

2.
a. The train was not late.
b. The train was late.
c. The train won't be late.
d. The train is also late.

7.
a. Who is studying at school?
b. What are you studying at school?
c. Where are you studying?
d. At which school are you studying?

3.
a. What is there?
b. What do you need?
c. Who is there?
d. What did you need?

8.
a. I work from 9 to 5.
b. Who works from 9 to 5?
c. Where do you work from 9 to 5?
d. From what time to what time
   do you work?

4.
a. It's raining today, too.
b. It's not raining today.
c. It was raining today.
d. It was not raining today.

9.
a. I give this to you.
b. To whom shall I give this?
c. Did I give this to you?
d. What did I give to you?

5
a. Where did you write a letter?
b. Who wrote a letter?
c. What did you write a letter with?
d. On which paper did you write a letter?

10.
a. I wrote this on the paper.
b. Who wrote this on the paper?
c. What did I write on the paper?
d. Where did I write this.

Evaluation: Speaking 1

Evaluation: Speaking   2

Scoring guide: date _____ name _____

a. Vocabulary: variety, new words	0 1 2 3 4
b. Sentence: variety, new structures	0 1 2 3 4
c. Attitude: gesture, eye contact	0 1 2 3 4
d. Voice: clear and natural	0 1 2 3 4
e. Memorized?	0 1 2 3 4

Your total points _____ / 20 _____

Evaluation: Reading and writing

1. A driver carried the luggage to the station.
   うんてんしゅ（　　）えき（　　）にもつ（　　）はこびました。
2. A dog entered the box.
   いぬ（　　）はこ（　　）はいりました。
3. Let's put the shoes on the floor.
   ゆか（　　）くつ（　　）おきましょう。
4. Please take the books out of your car.
   くるま（　　）ほん（　　）だして　ください。
5. Where did you put the photo in?
   しゃしん（　　）どこ（　　）いれましたか。
6. Shall we call the bank?
   ぎんこう（　　）でんわ（　　）かけましょうか。
7. Please write your name on this paper.
   このかみ（　　）あなたの　なまえ（　　）かいて　ください。
8. Let's go out.
   そと（　　）でましょう。
9. Let's ask to the store clerk.
   てんいん（　　）ききましょう。
10. Let's ride a bicycle.
    じてんしゃ（　　）のりましょう。
11. Give your telephone number to the teacher.
    せんせい（　　）でんわばんごう（　　）いって　ください。
12. Whom did you meet?
    あなたは　だれ（　　）あいましたか。

Page 116

おおきな くりの きの した で

あなた と わたし

いっしょに あそびましょう

おおきな くりの きの した で

ōkina kuri no ki no shita de	Under the big chestnut tree
anata to watashi	You and I
issho ni asobimasho	Let's play together
ōkina kuri no ki no shita de	Under the big chestnut tree

1. Make origami trees.
On the tree, draw fruits or leaves. What do you like to do under the tree?
Make a poster using the tree.

2. Conversation
A: だれと だれが あそびますか。
   dare to dare ga asobimasu ka. Who plays with whom?
B: (ともだち)と (せんせい)が あそびます。
   (tomodachi) to (sensei)ga asobimasu. My friend and the teacher play.

3. Useful expression
いっしょに (あそび)ましょう。
Issho ni (asobi)masho. Let's play together.

おおきな	くり	き	した	あなた	わたし	いっしょに	あそびましょう
ōkina	*kuri*	*ki*	*shita*	*anata*	*watashi*	*issho ni*	*asobimashō*
big	chestnut	tree	under	you	I	together	let's play

Page 117

Lesson 5: i-adjective, na-adjective, want to do

1. The teacher is holding two books.

One is "Nihon no Ocha", 2000, 500 yen, published in Japan. It is small, light, easy to read and interesting. The other book is: "American Maps", 1955, $20, published in the USA. It is big, heavy, difficult to read and not interesting.

A: <u>Atarashii</u> hon wa dore desu ka. あたらしい　ほんは　どれですか。	Which is the <u>new</u> book?
B: <u>Sore</u> desu. それです。	It's <u>that one</u>.

Substitute: old, big, small, difficult, heavy, inexpensive, easy, light

2. Vocabulary: i-adjectives

new, fresh	atarashii	あたらしい
old	hurui	ふるい
big	ōkii	おおきい
small	chiisai	ちいさい
inexpensive	yasui	やすい
expensive, high	takai	たかい
heavy	omoi	おもい
light	karui	かるい
easy	yasashii	やさしい
difficult	muzukashii	むずかしい
interesting	omoshiroi	おもしろい
uninteresting	tsumaranai	つまらない

3. Now you have the same books.

The teacher has never seen them before and is curious.

> A: Sono hon wa <u>yasui</u> desu ka, <u>takai</u> desu ka. Is that book <u>cheap</u> or
> その　ほんは　やすいですか、たかいですか。　　expensive?
>
> B: <u>Takai</u> desu.　　　　　　　　　　　　It's <u>expensive</u>.
> たかいです。

Substitute: heavy or light, easy or difficult, big or small, new or old

4. The books are off in separate corners of the room.

The teacher notices one and asks you about it.

> A: Ano hon wa <u>omoshiroi</u> desu ka, <u>omoshiroku</u> arimasen ka.
> あの　ほんは　おもしろいですか、おもしろく　ありませんか。
> 　　　　　　　　　　　　　Is that book over there <u>interesting</u> or not?
> B: <u>Omoshiroku</u> arimasen.　It's not <u>interesting</u>.
> おもしろく　ありません。

Substitute: easy, new, light, old, difficult, expensive, uninteresting

5. You just returned from a trip to Japan.

Your teacher is asking about your trip.

> A: <u>Ryokan</u> wa <u>yokatta</u> desu ka.　　　Was the <u>inn good</u>?
> りょかんは　よかったですか。
>
> B: <u>Yokatta</u> desu.　　　　　　　　　It was <u>good</u>.
> よかったです。

Substitute: bath (ohuro) - hot, meal (shokuji) - delicious,
water - cold, trip - enjoyable, town - old, friend - good

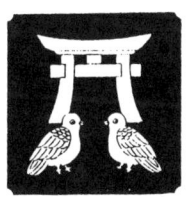

6. Vocabulary: i adjectives

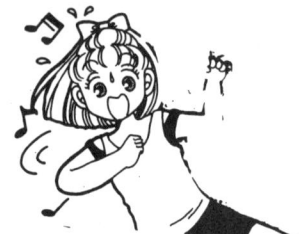

good	ii, yoi	いい、よい
hot	atsui	あつい
delicious	oishii	おいしい
cold	tsumetai	つめたい
enjoyable	tanoshii	たのしい

7. Take a trip with Bob to Mt. Fuji.

He is busy preparing, then goes by train, by bus, and finally by foot.
Afterwards he relaxes at a nearby hotspring.

A: Bob san wa isogashii desu ka.	Is Bob busy?
ボブさんは　いそしがしいですか。	
B: Isogashii desu.	He is busy.
いそがしいです。	

Substitute: Bob - busy, Mt. Fuji - far, Bullet train - fast, bus - slow
mountain - dangerous, shoes - dirty, mountain - cold

8. Vocabulary: i adjectives

busy	isogashii	いそがしい
far	tōi	とおい
fast	hayai	はやい
slow	osoi	おそい
dangerous	abunai	あぶない
dirty	kitanai	きたない
cold	samui	さむい
warm	attakai	あったかい
rare	mezurashii	めずらしい
near	chikai	ちかい

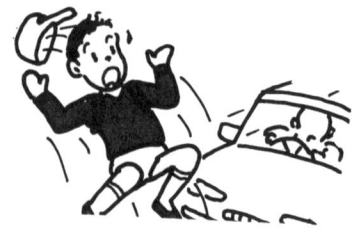

Page 120

9. The teacher wants to know how your trip to Mt. Fuji was.

A: Fuji san wa chikakatta desu ka, chikaku arimasen deshita ka.
ふじさんは　ちかかったですか、ちかく　ありませんでしたか。

Was Mt. Fuji near, or not?

B: Chikaku arimasen deshita.　　　It wasn't near.
ちかく　ありませんでした。

Substitute: bus - fast, mountain - warm, temple - rare, store - new
bus stop - near, hotspring - far, Bob - dirty, shoes - dirty

10. You have several shirts made of colored paper.
The teacher would llike to have one.

Sono akai shatsu o onegai shimasu.　　May I have that red shirt?
その　あかい　シャツを　おねがい　います。

Substitute: red, blue, yellow, black, white

11. Vocabulary: colors

red	akai	あかい
black	kuroi	くろい
white	shiroi	しろい
blue	aoi	あおい
yellow	kiiroi	きいろい

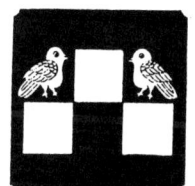

12. Pattern Drill: i-adjective conjugation

A: Atsui desu ka.	あついですか。
B: Atsuku arimasen.	あつく　ありません。
A: Kinō atsukatta desu ka.	きのう　あつかった　ですか。
B: Atsuku arimasen deshita.	あつく　ありませんでした。

Substitute: hot, busy, cold, dirty, slow, far, dangerous, good

Grammar: _i_- adjectives, _na_- adjectives, nouns

There are two kinds of adjectives: _i_ - adjectives and _na_ - adjectives

1. い adjective : All the adjectives which end with い
     chiisai, hurui, takai, omoshiroi, atsui, chikai, abunai, shiroi

2. な adjective
   a. Adjectives which do not end with い.
     shizuka, hima, daijōbu, kantan, hitsuyō, genki, suki,
   b. Some な adjectives end with い but they are な adjectives.
     kirei, yūmei, kirai

When _i_ - adjectives, _na_ - adjectives and nouns modify a noun,
the attachments are different.

1. い adjective :

chiisai machi	a small town
chiisai no	a small one
Ōkii hon o kaimashita.	I bought a large book.
Chiisai no o kaimashita ka.	Did you buy a small one?

2. な adjective:

shizuka na machi	a quiet town
shizuka na no	a quiet one
kirei na ie	a pretty house
kirei na no	a pretty one
Suki na hon wa kore desu.	My favorite book is this one.
Suki na no wa dore desu ka.	Which is your favorite one?

3. Noun:

watashi no hon	my book
watashi no	mine
Nihongo no hon wa kore desu.	The Japanese book is this one.
100 en no o kaimashita.	I bought the 100 yen (book).

Grammar: Conjugation of i-adjective and na-adjectives

i-adjectives: final -i becomes - ku arimasen, -katta desu.

ōkii machi	a big town
Ōkii desu.	It's big.
Ōkiku arimasen.	It isn't big.
Ōkikatta desu.	It was big.
Ōkiku arimasen deshita.	It wasn't big.

na-adjectives: similar to noun conjugation

shizuka na gakusei	a quiet student
Shizuka desu.	He is quiet.
Shukaka ja arimasen.	He isn't quiet.
Shizuka deshita.	He was quiet.
Shizuka ja arimasen deshita.	He wasn't quiet.

noun:

100 en no hon	a 100 yen book
100 en desu.	It is 100 yen.
100 en ja arimasen.	It isn't 100 yen.
100 en deshita.	It was 100 yen.
100 en ja arimasen deshita.	It wasn't 100 yen.

Grammar: I want to -- : (verb stem) + tai desu.

The -tai form is made by replacing -masu with -tai.
It is conjugated just like an i-adjective.

tabetai mono	Things I want to eat
tabe masu.	I eat.
tabetai desu.	I want to eat.
tabetaku arimasen.	I don't want to eat.
tabetakatta desu.	I wanted to eat.
tabetaku arimasen deshita.	I didn't want to eat.

13. The teacher wants to do something

and wonders if you would like to, also.

A: Watashi wa <u>Kyōto e ikimasu</u>.　I'm <u>going to Kyoto</u>.
　わたしは　きょうとへ　いきます。
　 Ann san mo <u>ikitai</u> desu ka.　　 Do you also want to <u>go</u>, Ann?
　 アンさんも　いきたい　ですか。

B: Hai, <u>ikitai</u> desu.　　　　　 Yes, I want to <u>go</u>.
　 はい、いきたいです。

Substitute: go to Kyoto, buy newspaper, look at garden, read here

14. You have no desire to do anything.

A: Kyō <u>hatarakitai</u> desu ka.　　Do you want to <u>work</u> today?
　 きょう　はたらきたいですか。

B: <u>Hatarakitaku</u> arimasen.　　　 I don't want to <u>work</u>.
　 はたらきたく　ありません。

A: Kinō <u>hatarakitakatta</u> desu ka.　Did you want to <u>work</u> yesterday?
　 きのう　はたらきたかった　ですか。

B: <u>Hatarakitaku</u> arimasen deshita.　I didn't want to <u>work</u>.
　 はたらきたく　ありません　でした。

Substitute:　write a letter, meet friend, buy a ticket, return to Japan

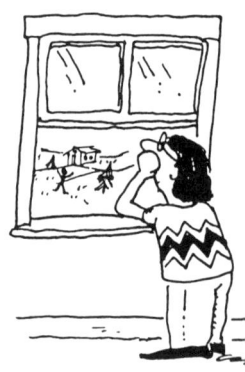

15. In that case let's find out what you want to do.

A: Ann san wa nani o shitai desu ka.	What do you want to do, Ann?
アンさんは　なにを　したいですか。	
B: <u>Otera e iki</u>tai desu.	I want to <u>go to the temple</u>.
おてらへ　いきたいです。	

Substitute: make sushi, take pictures, give it to the students

16. Practice with na-adjectives. Give any answers you like.

1.

A: <u>Suki</u> na mono wa nan desu ka.	What's your <u>favorite</u> thing?
すきな　ものは　なんですか。	
B: <u>Osushi</u> desu.	It's <u>sushi.</u>
おすしです。	

Substitute: important - ticket, necessary - address, convenient - car

2.

A: <u>Shizuka</u> na tokoro wa doko desu ka.	Where is a <u>quiet</u> palace?
しずかな　ところは　どこですか。	
B: <u>Niwa</u> desu.	It's a <u>garden</u>.
にわです。	

Substitute: famous - Kyoto, pretty - mountain, safe - this town

3.

A: <u>Hima</u> na hito wa dare desu ka.	Who is a <u>free</u> person?
ひまな　ひとは　だれですか。	
B: <u>Bob san</u> desu.	It's <u>Bob</u>.
ボブさんです。	

Substitute: kind - teacher, healthy - friend, pretty - my friend

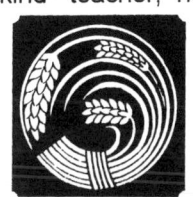

Page 125

17. Vocabulary: na-adjective

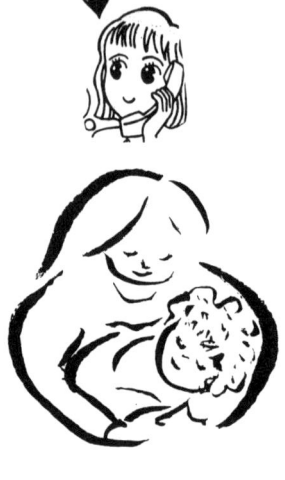

favorite	suki	すき
pretty, clean	kirei	きれい
convenient	benri	べんり
important	daiji	だいじ
necessary	hitsuyō	ひつよう
quiet	shizuka	しずか
famous	yūmei	ゆうめい
not busy, free	hima	ひま
kind	shinsetsu	しんせつ
healthy	genki	げんき
very much liked	daisuki	だいすき
safe	daijōbu	だいじょうぶ
simple	kantan	かんたん
thing	mono	もの
place	tokoro	ところ
person	hito	ひと
a meal	shokuji	しょくじ
garden	niwa	にわ
bath	ohuro	おふろ

18. The teacher is describing what she wants to see.

Ann san no kirei na akai yōhuku o misete kudasai.

Please show me Ann's pretty, red clothes.

アンさんの きれいな あかい ようふくを みせて ください。

Substitute: Bob's blue Japanese necktie, Ann's convenient little hand bag, teacher's yellow simple car, the driver's black important book

Grammar: Word order with several modifiers

There is no definite word order. All the expressions mean the same.
- a. Ann san no akai kirei na yōhuku
- b. akai Ann san no kirei na yōhuku
- c. kirei na akai Ann san no yōhuku
- d. Ann san no kirei na akai yōhuku

19. Pattern Drill: na-adjective conjugation

A: <u>Hima</u> desu ka. ひまですか。	Is he <u>free</u>?
B: <u>Hima</u> ja arimasen. ひまじゃ　ありません。	He's not free.
A: Kinō, <u>hima</u> deshita ka. きのう　ひまでしたか。	Was he free yesterday?
B: <u>Hima</u> ja arimasen deshita. ひまじゃ　ありません　でした。	He wasn't free.

Substitute: healthy, kind, pretty, famous, healthy, simple

20. How is your school?

A: <u>Gakkō</u> wa dō desu ka. がっこうは　どうですか。	How is <u>your school</u>?
B: <u>Tanoshii</u> desu. たのしいです。	It's <u>fun</u>.

Substitute: teacher - kind, Japanese book - easy, friend - interesting
book - simple, Japanese - difficult, study - enjoyable

21. Ask each other about your trip to Japan.

A: <u>Ryokō</u> wa dō deshita ka. りょこうは　どうでしたか。	How was <u>your trip</u>?
B: <u>Omoshiro</u>katta desu. おもしろかった　です。	It was <u>interesting.</u>

Substitute: inn - pretty, hotspring - hot, town - quiet, airplane - fast
ticket - expensive, meal - delicious, store clerk - kind, fish - rare

Page 127

LET'S PRACTICE SOME MORE.
もっと れんしゅう しましょう。
See Introductory lesson for details.

Vocabulary builders

1. Make cards
2. Listen and stand up
3. Listen and line up
4. Spread on the table
5. Shoots and ladders
6. Around the world

Quick draw + Full house bingo

Expressions

1. Sensei no chiisai tokei wa hurui desu.
2. Tomodachi no ōkii kutsu wa kitanaku arimasen.
3. Ginkōin no benri na kuruma wa takai desu.
4. Tenin no yasui yōhuku wa yoku arimsen.
5. Untenshu no takai ie wa kirei desu.
6. Hayai densha de tōi yama e ikimashita.
7. Tomodachi no ōkii <u>party</u> wa tanoshikatta desu.
8. Atarashii mise de shinsetsu na tomodachi ni aimashita.
9. Kitanai yōhuku o omoi nimotsu ni iremashita.
10. Kantan na kamera o chikai machi de kaimashita.

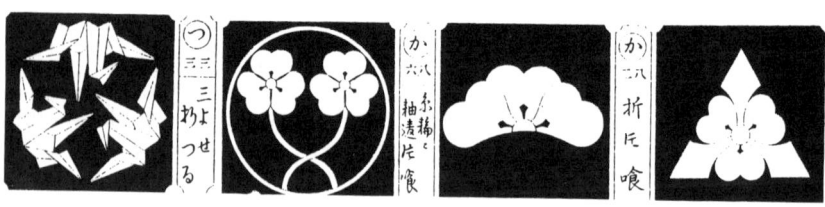

Change positive and negative

1. Kono gakkō wa ōkii desu.
2. Ano tokei wa huruku arimasen.
3. Gakusei no hon wa kantan ja arimasen.
4. Sensei no jisho wa daiji desu.
5. Nihongo no sensei wa Amerikajin ja arimasen.
6. Eigo no sensei wa Nihonjin desu.
7. Watashi wa okashi o tabetai desu.
8. Tomodachi ni denwa o kaketaku arimasen.
9. Kinō wa atsukatta desu.
10. Kinō wa shizuka ja arimasen deshita.
11. Kinō wa isogashiku arimasen deshita.
12. Kinō wa kirei deshita.
13. Kinō wa benkyō shitakatta desu.
14. Kinō wa hatarakitaku arimasen deshita.

Two way bingo

Basic sentences
1. Watashi wa isogashii desu.

a: busy, healthy, want to speak, fast
b: *postive, negative,   past,   past negative*

2. Isogashii hito ga mezurashii tokoro ni imasu.

a: busy, free, kind, big
b: warm, good, ineresting, new

3. Watashi wa ii niku o tabe tai desu.

a: good meat, clean vegetable, fresh fish, old cake
b: eat, buy, give, receive

4. Kinō tomodachi ni aitakatta desu.

a: kind teacher, good friend, my favorite student, busy clerk
b: meet, speak, call, · teach

Guessing game
Use i-adjectives and na-adjectives.

1. Sono hon wa <u>takai</u> desu ka.

i-adj.: (   ) (   ) (   )
na-adj:(   ) (   ) (   )

2. Kinō sono gakusei wa <u>genki</u> deshita ka.

i-adj.: (   ) (   ) (   )
na-adj:(   ) (   ) (   )

3. Suki na mono wa <u>ōkii</u> hon desu ka.

i-adj.: (   ) (   ) (   )
na-adj:(   ) (   ) (   )

4. Tanoshii tokoro wa <u>chikai</u> koen desu ka.

i-adj.: (   ) (   ) (   )
na-adj:(   ) (   ) (   )

5. Isogashii hito wa <u>shinsetsu na</u> gakusei desu ka.

i-adj.: (   ) (   ) (   )
na-adj:(   ) (   ) (   )

6. Anata wa ima <u>suwari</u> tai desu ka.

verb: (   ) (   ) (   )
      (   ) (   ) (   )

7. Tomodachiwa kinō <u>aruki</u> takatta desu ka.

verb: (   ) (   ) (   )
      (   ) (   ) (   )

About myself

1. Watashi wa hima na gakusei desu.
2. Kinō wa isogashiku arimasen deshita.
3. Watashi wa Nihon no ocha ga daisuki desu.
4. Watashi wa ōkii jisho ga hitsuyō desu.
5. Watashi no heya wa yoku arimasen.
6. Atatakai tokoro ni sumitai desu.
7. Ima tomodachi ni denwa o kaketaku arimasen.
8. Kirei na yōhuku to kutsu o kaitai desu.
9. Hikōki de Nihon e ikitaku arimasen.
10. Nihongo o mainichi hanashitai desu.

Interview

Examples:
1. Anata wa ima isogashii desu ka, isogashiku arimsen ka.
2. Anata no suki na mono wa nan desu ka.
3. Anata no ie wa shizuka desu ka, shizuka ja ariamsen ka.
4. Anata no gakkō wa dō desu ka.
5. Kinō no nihongo no benkyō wa dō deshita ka.
6. Kinō anata no ie wa shizuka deshita ka.
7. Suki na tokoro wa doko desu ka.
8. Kono shokuji wa oishikatta desu ka.
9. Nani o shitai desu ka.
10. Kinō wa dō deshita ka.
11. Nan no benkyō ga daiji desu ka.
12. Nan no hon o yomitai desu ka.
13. Dare to issho ni hanashitai desu ka.
14. Ōkii kaisha de hatarakitai desu ka.

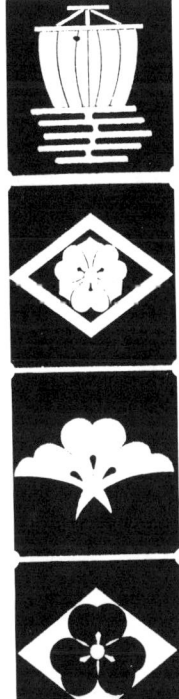

Page 131

Constructing a sentence

1. Which is the interesting book?
   か、は、おもしろい、どれ、ほん、です

2. That telephone is expensive.
   です、たかい、は、でんわ、その

3. Those clothes over there are not new.
   あたらしく、ようふく、ありません、は、あの

4. The meal was delicious.
   おいしかった、しょくじ、です、は

5. The trip was not enjoyable.
   ありません、たのしく、は、りょこう、でした

6. I want to take pictures at the mountain.
   しゃしん、で、を、たいです、やま、とり

7. I don't want to teach English to the bank worker.
   たくありません、えいご、ぎんこういん、
   を、に、おしえ

8. My favorite thing isn't vegetables.
   わたし、すき、やさい、ありません、もの、
   の、な、は、じゃ

9. The school was quiet.
   しずか、でした、は、がっこう

10. The friend is not kind.
    じゃ、しんせつ、ともだち、ありません

Describe in Japanese.

1. kyō きょう

2. watashi わたし

3. Nihon にほん

4. watashi no gakkō わたしの　がっこう

5. Nihongo no kurasu にほんごの　クラス

6. watashi no tomodachi わたしの　ともだち

7. watashi no machi わたしの　まち

8. watashi no sensei わたしの　せんせい

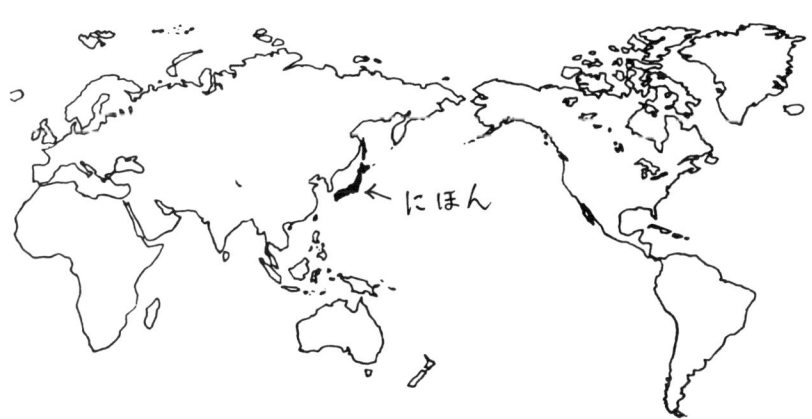

← にほん

A letter to your pen pal

こんにちは、みちよさん。 おげんきですか。
きょうは わたしの がっこうの ことを かきます。
わたしの がっこうの なまえは セントラル
こうこうです。
とても おおきい あたらしい きれいな
こうこうです。 しずかな べんりな ところに
あります。 まいにち たのしいです。
こうこうに いい おもしろい しんせつな
ともだちが います。 がっこうの べんきょうは
まいにち いそがしいですが わたしは すきです。
むずかしく ありません。 かんたんです。 がっこうの
ひるごはんは おいしいです。 わたしは あるいて
こうこうへ いきます。 わたしの いえから べんりな
ちかい ところに あります。

みちよさんの がっこうは どうですか。べんきょうは
どうですか。せんせいと ともだちは どうですか。
てがみを まって います。 さようなら。 ボブより

Answer the questions about this letter.

1・ボブさんの こうこうの なまえは なんですか。
2・その こうこうは どうですか。
3・どんな ともだちが いますか。
4・べんきょうは どうですか。
5・ボブさんは ひるごはんは すきですか。
6・ボブさんは なにで こうこうへ いきますか。
7・ボブさんの いえは どうですか。

Write a letter to a pen pal.

Evaluation: Listening comprehension

1.
a. This is an expensive car.
b. This is an old car.
c. This is a good car.
d. This is my favorite car.

6.
a. What's your favorite book?
b. What's your favorite car?
c. What's your favorite thing?
d. What's your favorite flower?

2.
a. The fish is delicious.
b. This fish isn't delicious.
c. The fish was delicious.
d. The fish wasn't delicious.

7.
a. Who is good?
b. Who isn't good?
c. Who was good?
d. Who wasn't good?

3.
a. The school is kind.
b. The school isn't kind.
c .The school was kind.
d. The school wasn't kind.

8.
a. Where do you want to go?
b. Who wants to go?
c. Which town do you want to visit?
d. Whose house do you want to visit?

4.
a. I want to go.
b. I don't want to go.
c. I wanted to go.
d..I didn't want to go.

9.
a. How is your trip?
b. How was your trip?
c. Was your trip good?
d. Is your trip good?

5
a. my small pretty new clothes
b. my big dirty old clothes
c. my expensive pretty new clothes
d. my heavy warm important clothes

10.
a. What do you want to do?
b. What do you want to read?
c. What do you want to buy?
d. What do you want to speak?

Evaluation: Speaking 1

Evaluation: Speaking 2

Scoring guide: date _____ name _____

a. Vocabulary: variety, new words	0 1 2 3 4
b. Sentence: variety, new structures	0 1 2 3 4
c. Attitude: gesture, eye contact	0 1 2 3 4
d. Voice: clear and natural	0 1 2 3 4
e. Memorized?	0 1 2 3 4

Your total points _____ / 20 _____

Evaluation: Reading and writing

1. I am eating delicious cake at a pretty store.
(   ) みせで (   ) おかしを たべて います。

2. I want to buy a new car at a convenient town.
(   ) まちで (   ) くるまを かいたいです。

3. I gave warm clothes to my favorite friend.
(   ) ともだちに (   ) ようふくを あげました。

4. There are expensive shoes in the famous store.
(   ) みせに (   ) くつが あります。

5. Please put this dirty vegetable in that old box.
その (   ) はこに この (   ) やさいを いれてください。

6. Where do you want to write your name and address?
なまえ (   ) じゅうしょ (   ) どこ (   ) かきたいですか。

7. Did you put your luggage on the floor?
にもつ (   ) ゆか (   ) おきましたか。

8. To whom did you say your phone number?
でんわばんごう (   ) だれ (   ) いいましたか。

Appendix 1: Map of Japan *Nihon no chizu*

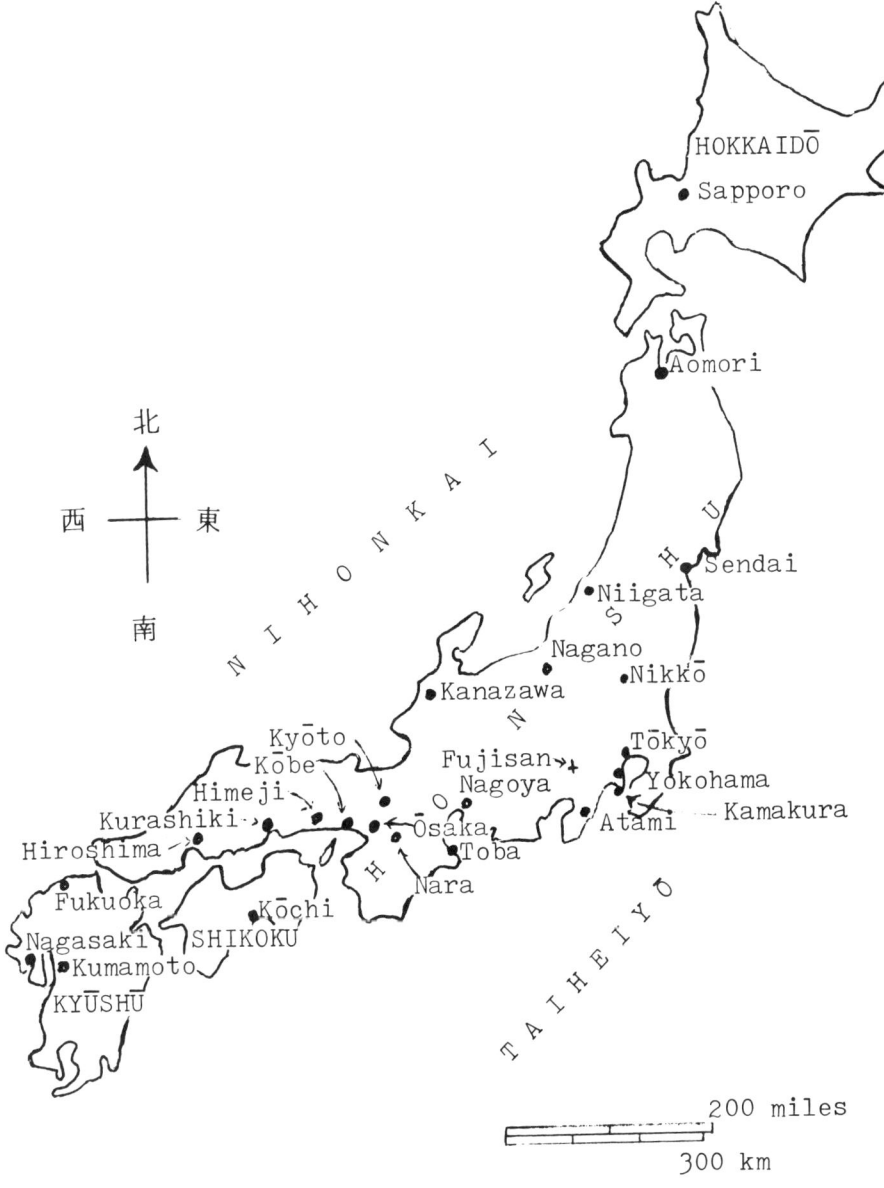

Appendix 2: Japanese holidays and annual events

Jan. 1-3	New Year's Day *Shōgatsu* Visit shrines & relatives in best kimono, eat special foods, read greeting cards, give-receive gift money. Play with tops, kites, card game, hanetsuki, fuku warai, sugoroku.
Jan. 2nd Monday	Coming-of-Age Day *Seijin no hi* Celebration for reaching at 20 years old To become self-reliant members of society.
Feb. 3/4	Bean-Throwing Ceremony *Setsubun* Make goblin masks. Throw soybeans shouting 'Out with the goblins and in with fortune!'
Feb. 11	National Foundation Day *Kenkoku kinenbi* Pray for the nation's happiness.
Mar. 3	Doll Festival *Hina matsuri, Momo no sekku* Decorate dolls, peach flowers & spring color. Cakes on a tiered platform covered with red felt.
Mar. 20	Spring Equinox Day *Shūnbun no hi* Plant flowers and vegetable.
April 29-May 5th	Golden Week A week long vacation time Take a trip, visit relatives, enjoy with family.
April 29	Greenery Day *Midori no hi* Go hiking. Picnic under the cherry blossoms: hanami
May 1	May Day, Company worker's day Workers unions have marches through towns.
May 3	Constitution Day *Kenpō kinenbi* The Constitution came in force on May 3, 1947, declares that sovereignty lies with the people.
May 5	Children's Day *Kodomo no hi* Celebrate the growth of children. Carp streamers swim vigorously in the blue sky. Eat kashiwamochi.
May 2nd Sunday	Mother's Day *Haha no hi* Appreciate mother's loving care to children. Make a mother's day card to express thankfulness.
June-July	Rainy season *Tsuyu* Wet muggy weather continues. This season helps plants grow and flourish.
July 7	The Star Festival *Tanabata* Altair and Vega are allowed to meet once a Year. Decorate bamboo branches with wishes written on paper strips.
July 20	Marine Day *Umi no hi* Japan is surrounded by the sea Food, scenery, Weather are Connected with the sea in daily base.
Aug. 6	Hiroshima day *Genbaku kinenbi* Atom bombs dropped. Praying for eternal peace at Hiroshima Peace Memorial Park.
mid-August	Ancestors' festival *Obon* Deceased reunite with their family. Visit graves, dance *Bon odori*. Set candles afloat in rivers.
Sept. 15	Respect-for-the Aged Day *Keiro no hi* Show respect to long-time Contributors to society & families. Pray for their health & longevity.
Fall full moon	Moon viewing night *Tsukimi* Decorate vegetable, fruit, full moon shaped Round rice cake & flowes on veranda. Enjoy poems & songs.
Sept. 23	Autumn Equinox Day *Shubun no hi* Pay respects to deceased family members.
Oct. 2nd Monday	Sports Day *Taiiku no hi* Schools, neighborhood communities and companies hold sports events.
Nov. 3	Culture Day *Bunka no hi* Art exhibition and music performance Present culture awards.
Nov. 15	7-5-3 years old celebration *Shichi go san* Pray at shrine. Eat longevity candy.
Nov. 23	Harvest Thanksgiving Day *Kinrō kansha no hi* Harvest festivals Enjoy freshly harvested rice & produce.
Dec. 23	Emperor's Birthday *Tennō tanjobi*
Dec. 25	Christmas Town and shops are busy with Santa and lights. Exchange presents.
Dec. 31	New Year's Eve *Ōmisoka* Clean your house, prepare for New Year. Eat long noodles, Temple bells ring 108 times at midnight: joya no kane

Appendix 3: Origami - flower tree bird fish frog

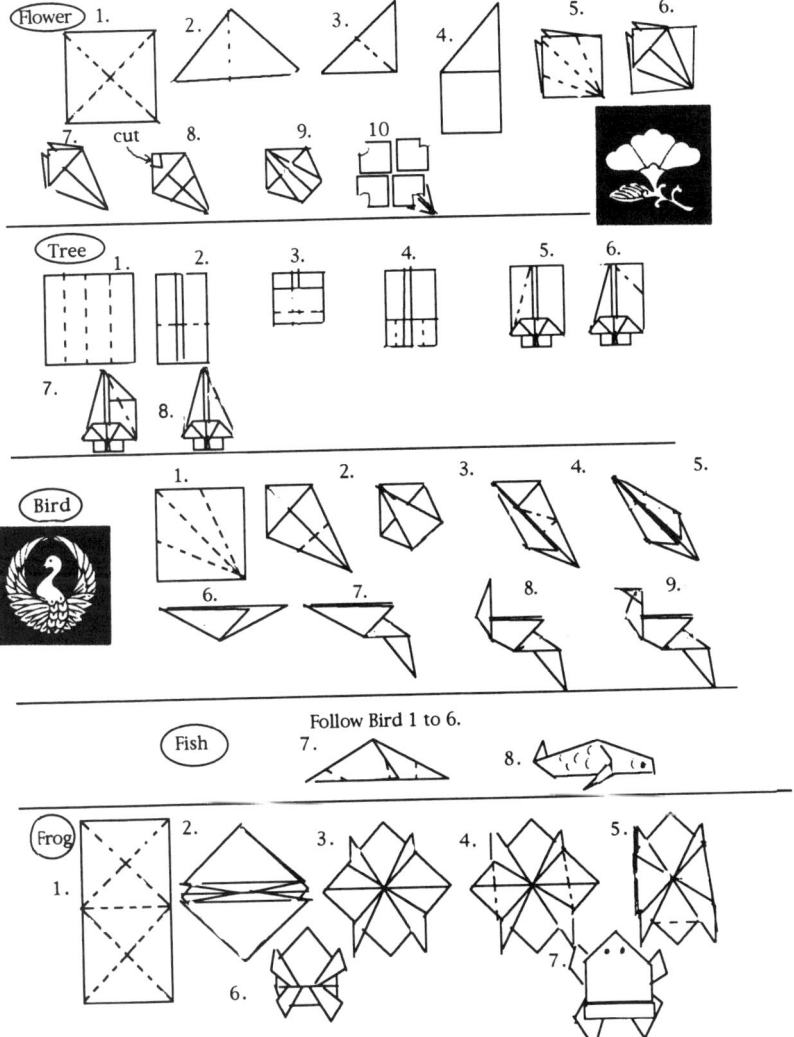

Appendix 4: Hiragana and Katakana Charts

Japanese has three writing systems: hiragana (phonetic), katakana (phonetic for foreign words), and kanji (Chinese characters) Hiragana is the first one taught in Japan.
Katakana is used to write foreign words and animal sounds and such.

Hiragana

a	i	u	e	o	
あ	い	う	え	お	
か	き	く	け	こ	k
さ	し	す	せ	そ	s
た	ち	つ	て	と	t
な	に	ぬ	ね	の	n
は	ひ	ふ	へ	ほ	h
ま	み	む	め	も	m
や	い	ゆ	え	よ	y
ら	り	る	れ	ろ	r
わ	い	う	え	を	w
ん					
が	ぎ	ぐ	げ	ご	g
ざ	じ	ず	ぜ	ぞ	z
だ	ぢ	づ	で	ど	d
ば	び	ぶ	べ	ぼ	b
ぱ	ぴ	ぷ	ぺ	ぽ	p

Katakana

a	i	u	e	o
ア	イ	ウ	エ	オ
カ	キ	ク	ケ	コ
サ	シ	ス	セ	ソ
タ	チ	ツ	テ	ト
ナ	ニ	ヌ	ネ	ノ
ハ	ヒ	フ	ヘ	ホ
マ	ミ	ム	メ	モ
ヤ	イ	ユ	エ	ヨ
ラ	リ	ル	レ	ロ
ワ	イ	ウ	エ	ヲ
ン				
ガ	ギ	グ	ゲ	ゴ
ザ	ジ	ズ	ゼ	ゾ
ダ	ヂ	ヅ	デ	ド
バ	ビ	ブ	ベ	ボ
パ	ピ	プ	ペ	ポ

Appendix 5: Contracted Hiragana and Katakana

	a	u	o
ky	きゃ・キャ	きゅ・キュ	きょ・キョ
sh	しゃ・シャ	しゅ・シュ	しょ・ショ
ch	ちゃ・チャ	ちゅ・チュ	ちょ・チョ
ny	みゃ・ミャ	みゅ・ミュ	みょ・ミョ
hy	ひゃ・ヒャ	ひゅ・ヒュ	ひょ・ヒョ
my	みゃ・ミャ	みゅ・ミュ	みょ・ミョ
ry	りゃ・リャ	りゅ・リュ	りょ・リョ
gy	ぎゃ・ギャ	ぎゅ・ギュ	ぎょ・ギョ
j	じゃ・ジュ	じゅ・ジュ	じょ・ジョ
j	ぢゃ・ヂャ	ぢゅ・ヂュ	ぢょ・ヂョ
by	びゃ・ビャ	びゅ・ビュ	びょ・ビョ
py	ぴゃ・ピャ	ぴゅ・ピュ	ぴょ・ピョ

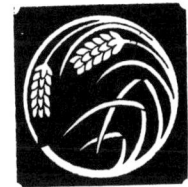

Appendix 6:   Hiragana Stroke Order

Make stokes from left to right, from top to bottom. The stroke order and direction are important.

a	あ	一	ナ	あ		ha	は	ｌ	ｌ-	は	
i	い	ｌ	い			hi	ひ	ひ	ひ		
u	う	ヽ	う			hu	ふ	ろ	ふ	ふ	
e	え	、	え			he	へ	へ			
o	お	一	ゐ	お		ho	ほ	ｌ	ｌ-	ｌ-	ほ
ka	か	つ	カ	か		ma	ま	一	＝	ま	
ki	き	一	＝	き	き	mi	み	み	み		
ku	く	く				mu	む	一	む	む	
ke	け	ｌ	ｌ-	け		me	め	ｌ	め		
ko	こ	つ	こ			mo	も	し	も	も	
sa	さ	一	さ	さ		ya	や	つ	か	や	
shi	し	し				yu	ゆ	ひ	ゆ		
su	す	一	す			yo	よ	一	よ		
se	せ	一	サ	せ		ra	ら	、	ら		
so	そ	、	ッ	そ		ri	り	ｌ	り		
ta	た	一	ナ	た	た	ru	る	る			
chi	ち	一	ち			re	れ	れ			
tsu	つ	つ				ro	ろ	ろ			
te	て	て				wa	わ	わ			
to	と	、	と			o	を	一	ち	を	
na	な	一	ナ	ナ	な	n	ん	ん			
ni	に	ｌ	ｌ-	に							
nu	ぬ	ｌ	ぬ								
ne	ね	ｌ	ね								
no	の	の									

Page 142

Appendix 7: Katakana Stroke Order

a	ア	フ	ア		ha	ハ	ノ	ハ			
i	イ	ノ	イ		hi	ヒ	ー	ヒ			
u	ウ	`	``	ウ	hu	フ	フ				
e	エ	ー	フ	エ	he	ヘ	ヘ				
o	オ	ー	ナ	オ	ho	ホ	ー	ナ	オ	ホ	
ka	カ	フ	カ		ma	マ	フ	マ			
ki	キ	ー	ニ	キ	mi	ミ	`	ニ	ミ		
ku	ク	ノ	ク		mu	ム	∠	ム			
ke	ケ	ノ	レ	ケ	me	メ	ノ	メ			
ko	コ	フ	コ		mo	モ	ー	ニ	モ		
sa	サ	ー	ナ	サ	ya	ヤ	フ	ヤ			
shi	シ	`	ニ	シ	yu	ユ	フ	ユ			
su	ス	フ	ス		yo	ヨ	フ	ヲ	ヨ		
se	セ	フ	セ		ra	ラ	ー	ラ			
so	ソ	`	ソ		ri	リ	l	リ			
ta	タ	ノ	ク	タ	ru	ル	)	ル			
chi	チ	ノ	ニ	チ	re	レ	レ				
tsu	ツ	`	``	ツ	ro	ロ	l	⼎	ロ		
te	テ	ー	ニ	テ	wa	ワ	l	ワ			
to	ト	l	ト		o	ヲ	フ	ヲ			
na	ナ	ー	ナ		n	ン	`	ン			
ni	ニ	ー	ニ								
nu	ヌ	フ	ヌ								
ne	ネ	`	フ	ネ	ネ						
no	ノ	)									

Page 143

Appendix 8: Fun With Kanji

Many years ago Chinese scholars created Kanji from the image of actual objects and concepts.

1. Fun with Chinese character: kanji

Kanji is fun to learn and beautiful to look at, often used in Japanese calligraphy as an art form. Take your time to look at the tone of the line: strong, weak, elegant, swift, sturdy, light, heavy, warm, cool,... Try to feel the artist's heart and mind. Now you are on the way to the center of Japanese culture.

2. Be a calligraphy artist.

For calligraphy use a sumi brush to write kanji. To begin with, prepare all the tools on your desk: ink, a brush, a sheet of rice paper on a mat, and kanji you like to write. Sit with good posture and relax. Close your eyes and take three deep breathes to center yourself into the art work you are about to do. Now begin to think about what you are going to write, for example, a tree,木. Think of a real tree. Look at the character 木. Rehearse the stroke order until you know it by heart. Finally begin to write it. Practice many times. Notice each 木 on the paper is talking to you. Put the best one on the wall.

3. Why Japanese uses Chinese characters?

The origin of spoken Chinese and Japanese are totally different, just like English and Japanese. In early time, Japanese did not have a writing system, but since Japan and China are located side by side and cultural exchange was frequent, Japanese borrowed Chinese characters and modified them in a Japanese way. Katakana and hiragana are a Japanese invention, modified from Chinese characters.

4. Origin of Chinese Characters

Kanji was born in ancient China. Chinese scholars created kanji from the image of actual objects and concepts. The best way for you to learn kanji is to begin with a character which has a clear image of an object.

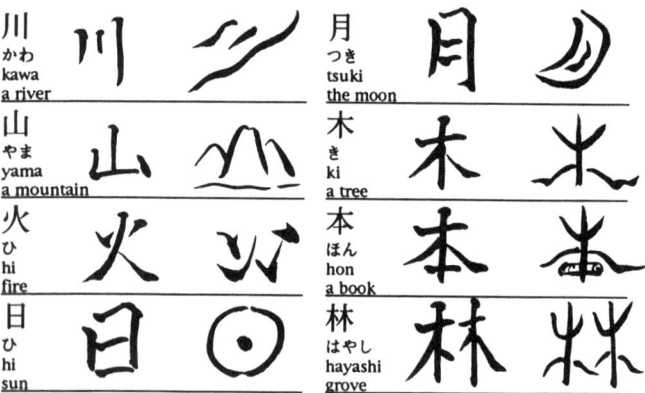

川
かわ
kawa
a river

月
つき
tsuki
the moon

山
やま
yama
a mountain

木
き
ki
a tree

火
ひ
hi
fire

本
ほん
hon
a book

日
ひ
hi
sun

林
はやし
hayashi
grove

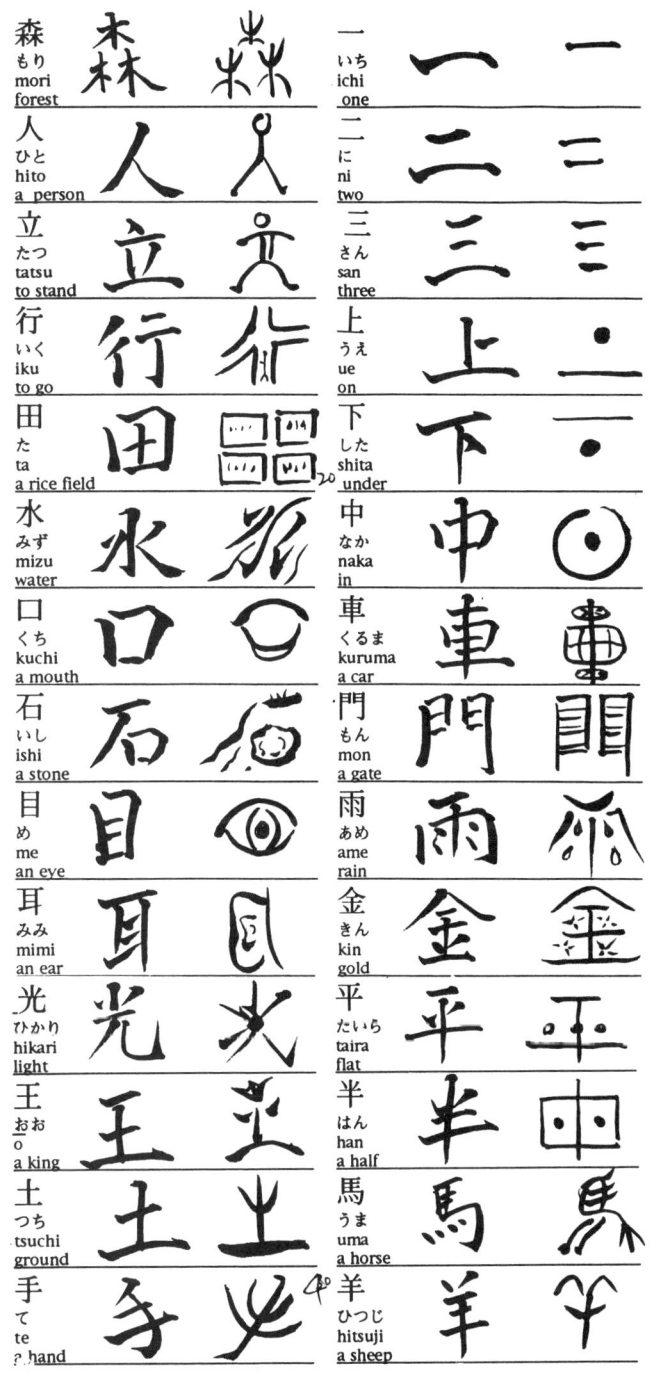

森
もり
mori
forest

人
ひと
hito
a person

立
たつ
tatsu
to stand

行
いく
iku
to go

田
た
ta
a rice field

水
みず
mizu
water

口
くち
kuchi
a mouth

石
いし
ishi
a stone

目
め
me
an eye

耳
みみ
mimi
an ear

光
ひかり
hikari
light

王
おお
o
a king

土
つち
tsuchi
ground

手
て
te
a hand

一
いち
ichi
one

二
に
ni
two

三
さん
san
three

上
うえ
ue
on

下
した
shita
under

中
なか
naka
in

車
くるま
kuruma
a car

門
もん
mon
a gate

雨
あめ
ame
rain

金
きん
kin
gold

平
たいら
taira
flat

半
はん
han
a half

馬
うま
uma
a horse

羊
ひつじ
hitsuji
a sheep

Appendix 9: Learning Through Actions

Learn Japanese with your whole body. Act out sentences in context without translating. Your ears and your whole body become involved in understanding Japanese. Here are the steps to learn action words:

1. The teacher says the sentences in various orders while acting them out. Listen and watch.
2. Act out sentence with the teacher.
3. Repeat after the teacher and act out after teacher.
4. Take the teacher's role if possible.

Action series

1. tachimasu   stand up   24. yakyū shimasu   play baseball
2. arukimasu   walk   25. tenisu shimasu   play tennis
3. hashirimasu   run   26. dansu shimasu   dance
4. tobimasu   jump   27. ryōri shimasu   cook
5. tomarimasu   stop   28. sentaku shimasu   do laundry
6. suwarimasu   sit down   29. unten shimasu   drive

7. tabemasu   eat   30. denwa o torimasu   pick up a phone
8. nomimasu   drink   31 denwa o kakemasu   dial a phone
9. nemasu   sleep   32. namae o iimasu   say a name
10. okimasu   get up   33. uta o utaimasu   sing a song
11. hatarakimasu work   34. piano o hikimasu   play the piano
12. yasumimasu   rest   35. denwa o okimasu   put down a phone

13. hanashimasu   speak   36. mise e ikimasu   go to a store
14. kikimasu   listen   37. koko e kimasu   come here
15. kakimasu   write   38. uchi e kaerimasu   go back home
16. yomimasu   read   39. yōhuku o kimasu   put on clothes
17. misemasu   show   40. kutsu o hakimasu   put on shoes
18. mimasu   look   41. kutsu o nugimasu   take off stockings

19. akemasu   open   42. bōshi o kaburimasu put on a hat
20. demasu   go out   43. tokei o shimasu   put on a watch
21. machimasu   wait   44. denki o tsukemasu turn on the light
22. hairimasu   enter   45. terebi o keshimasu turn off the T.V.
23. shimemasu   close   46. kagi o kakemasu   lock

Appendix 10: Conjugation - Noun, Verb, Adjectives

Noun: clerk	present	past
affirmative	tenin desu てんいんです	tenin deshita てんいんでした
negative	tenin ja arimasen てんいんじゃ ありません	tenin ja arimasen deshita てんいんじゃ ありません でした

Verb: eat	present	past
affirmative	tabemasu たべます	tabemasen たべません
negative	tabemashita たべました	tabemasen deshita たべません でした

Na-adj: free	present	past
affirmative	hima desu ひまです	hima deshita ひまでした
negative	hima ja arimasen ひまじゃ ありません	hima ja arimasen deshita ひまじゃ ありません でした

I-adj: big	present	past
affirmative	okii desu おおきいです	okikatta desu おおきかったです
negative	okiku arimasen おおきく ありません	okiku arimasen deshita おおきく ありません でした

want to: look	present	past
affirmative	mitai desu みたいです	mitakatta desu みたかったです
negative	mitaku arimasen みたく ありません	mitaku arimasen deshita みたく ありませんでした

Appendix 11: Verbs Organized By *Te* Form Patterns

-te

give	there is
ageru	iru
agemasu	imasu
agete	ite
open	put in
akeru	ireru
akemasu	iremasu
akete	irete
take out	call/hang
dasu	kakeru
dashimasu	kakemasu
dashite	kakete
able to do	visible
dekiru	mieru
dekimasu	miemasu
dekite	miete
go out	look
deru	miru
demasu	mimasu
dete	mite
come	show
kuru	miseru
kimasu	misemasu
kite	misete
wear	be late
kiru	okureru
kimasu	okuremasu
kite	okurete
speak	get down
hanasu	oriru
hanashimasu	orimasu
hanashite	orite

teach	
oshieru	
oshiemasu	
oshiete	
do	
suru	
shimasu	
shite	
close	
shimeru	
shimemasu	
shimete	
eat	
taberu	
tabemasu	
tabete	
get tired	
tsukareru	
tsukaremasu	
tsukarete	

-tte

meet	
au	
aimasu	
atte	
there is	
aru	
arimasu	
atte	
enter	
hairu	
hairimasu	
haitte	
pay	
harau	
haraimasu	
haratte	
rain	
huru	
hurimasu	
hutte	
say	
iu	
iimasu	
itte	
go	
iku	
ikimasu	
itte	
need	
iru	
irimasu	
itte	

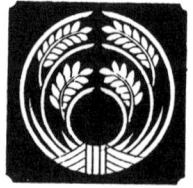

go back	stand up	-ite walk	-nde carry
kaeru	tatsu	aruku	hakobu
kaerimasu	tachimasu	arukimasu	hakobimasu
kaette	tatte	aruite	hakonde
buy	stop	put on foot	drink
kau	tomaru	haku	nomu
kaimasu	tomarimasu	hakimasu	nomimasu
katte	tomatte	haite	nonde
wait	take	write	live
matsu	toru	kaku	sumu
machimasu	torimasu	kakimasu	sumimasu
matte	totte	kaite	sunde
hold	make	hear	read
motsu	tsukuru	kiku	yomu
mochimasu	tsukurimasu	kikimasu	yomimasu
motte	tsukutte	kiite	yonde

receive
morau
moraimasu
moratte

put
oku
okimasu
oite

get on
noru
norimasu
notte

arrive
tsuku
tsukimasu
tsuite

take off
nugu
nugimasu
nuide

put away
shimau
shimaimasu
shimatte

work
hataraku
hatarakimasu
hataraite

sit down
suwaru
suwarimasu
suwatte

Appendix 12: Particles

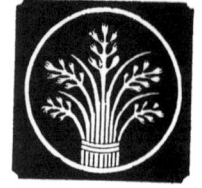

1. は / wa   theme, topic   Kippu wa 100 en desu.
     as for -   *As for the ticket, it is 100 yen.*
2. か / ka   question mark   Kore wa chizu desu ka.
     Is this a map?
3. の / no   modifier, apostrophe-s   Ocha no hon o kudasai.
     of -   *Please give the a book on tea.*
4. へ / e   direction   Umi e ikimashō.
     to - , towards -   *Let's go to the sea.*
5. で / de   transportation, instrument   Kuruma de kaerimasu.
     by means of -   *I return by car.*
6. と / to   noun *and* noun   Sakana to niku o tabemasu.
     I eat fish and meat.
7. が / ga   *- but*   Hon wa irimasu ga pen wa iriasen.
     I need books but not pens.
8. を / o   direct object   Watashi wa hikōki o mimashita
     I saw an airplane.
9. で / de   location of action   Machi de hatarakimasu.
     at - , in -   *I work in town.*
10. が / ga   emphasis to the subject   Dare ga sensei desu ka.
     Who is the teacher?
     Bob ga sensei desu.
     Bob is a teacher.
11. に / ni   goal of action   Tōkyō ni tsukimashita.
     I arrived in Tokyo.
     place of existence   Neko wa niwa ni imasu.
     A cat is in the garden.
     point of time   Jū ji ni nemasu.
     I go to sleep at 10.
12. から / kara   *from -*   Nihon kara kimashita.
     I came from Japan.
13. まで / made   *until - , up to -*   Go ji made hatarakimasu.
     I work until 5.
14. も / mo   *also, too*   Neko ga imasu. Inu mo imasu.
     There is a cat. There is a dog, too.

Appendix 13: Glossary: Japanese to English

A:
abunai:dangerous
aimasu:atte:au: to meet
akai:red
akemasu:akete:akeru:
    to open
ame:rain
amerika:America
anata:you
annaisho:information
    center
ano:that+noun
aoi:blue
are:that one
arigato:thank you
arigato gozaimasu:
    Thank you very much.
arimasu:atte:aru:
    there is..
arukimasu:aruite:aruku:
    to walk
ashita:tomorrow
asoko:over there
atarashii:new,fresh
atatakai:warm
atsui:hot
attakai:warm

B:
basu:bus
basu noriba:bus stop
benjo:restroom
benkyo:study(noun)
benri:handy,
biiru:beer

C:
cha:tea
chiisai:small
chikai:near,close
chizu:map
chotto:a little, a few

D:
daiji:important, precious
daijobu:no problem
daisuki:very much pleasing
dare:who
dashimasu:dashite:dasu:
    to take out
de:by means of
de:at,in, on
dekimasu:dekite,dekiru:
    to be able to
demasu:dete:deru:
    to go out
denwa:telephone
denwa bango:tel.number
denwa bokkusu:tel.booth
deshita:It was..
desu:It is..
do:how
doko:where
donata:who
dono:which+(noun)
dore:which one
doru:dollar

E:
e:to
eigo:English
eki:station
en:yen

Page 151

G:
ga:(subject marker)
ga:but
gakkō:school
gakusei:student
genki:healthy
ginkō:bank
ginkōin:bank worker
gochisōsama:(see intro.)
gohan:meal,rice
gomen kudasai:(see intro.)

H:
hachi:8
hai:yes
hairimasu:haitte:hairu:
    to enter
hajime ni:at first
hakimasu:haite:haku:
    to wear (on foot)
hako:box
hakobimasu:hakonde:hakobu:
    to carry
hana:flower
hanashimasu:hanashite:hanasu
    to speak
haraimasu:haratte:harau:
    to pay
hatarakimasu:hataraite:
    hataraku: to work
hayai:speedy,early
heya:room
hikōki:airplane
hima:freetime
hito:person
hitsuyō:necessary
hon:book
hune:ship,boat
hurimasu:hutte:huru:
    to rain
huro:bath
hurui:old
hyaku:100

I:
ichi:1
ie:house
ii:good
iie:no
iimasu:itte:iu:to say
ikaga:how
ikimasu:itte:iku:to go
ikura:how much
ima:now
imasu:ite:iru:there is
ippai:a containerful
irasshaimase:welcome
irimasu:itte:iru:to need
iremasu:irete:ireru:
    to put in
isogimasu:isoide:isogu:
    to hurry
issho ni:togethere
isu:chair
itadakimasu:(see intro.)
itsumo:always
itte mairimasu:(see intro
itte rasshai:(see intro.)

J:
ja:well, then
ja arimasen:it is not
ji:o'clock
jisho:dictionary
jitensha:bicycle
jūsho:adress
jū:10

K:
ka:(question marker)
kaerimasu:kaette:kaeru:
   to go back/return
kaimasu:katte:kau:to buy
kaisha:company
kakekata:way of telephoning
kakemasu:kakete:kakeru:
   to telephone
kakimasu:kaite:kaku:
   to write
kami:paper
kane:money
kara:from
karui:light weight
kiiroi:yellow
kikimasu:kiite:kiku:
   to listen/to ask
kimasu:kite:kuru:to come
kimasu:kite:kiru:to wear
kinō:yesterday
kippu:ticket
kirei:pretty,clean
kitanai:dirty
kochira e:to this way
kōhi:coffee
koko:here,this place
konnichiwa:hellow
konbanwa:good evening
kono:this+(noun)
kore:this one
kudasai:Give me
kūkō:airport
kuroi:black
kuruma:car
kutsu:shoes
kyō:today
kyū:9
kekkō:fine

M:
machi:town
machimasu:matte:matsu:
   to wait
made:until,up to
mainichi:everyday
man:10000
masen:do not
masen deshita:did not
mashita:did
mashō:Let's/ I'll
mashō ka:shall we/shall I
masu:do
mata:again
matte kudasai:Please waite
mezurashii:rare,unusual
miemasu:miete:mieru:
   to be visible
mimasu:mite:miru:to see
miruku:milk
mise:store
misemasu:misete:miseru:
   to show
mizu:water(cold)
mo:also,too
mochimasu:motte:motsu:
   to hold/have
mō ichido:once more
mono:thing
moraimasu:moratte:morau:
   to receive
muzukashii:difficult

N:
nan/nani:what
nana:7
ne:isn't it?
neko → ni:at,on,in
cat   ni:2
nihon:Japan
nihonjin:Japanese person
nihongo:japanese language
niku:meat

nimotsu:luggage
niwa:garden
no:'s
nomimasu:nonde:nomu:
    to drink
norimasu:notte:noru:
    to ride,/get on
nugimasu:nuide:nugu:
    to take off

O:
o:direct object marker
ocha:tea
ohuro:bath
oishii:delicious
okane:money
okashi:cake
ōkii:big
okimasu:oite:oku:
    to put
okimasu:okite:okiru:
    to get up
okuremasu:okurete:okureru
    to be late
omiyage:souvenir
omoi:heavy
omoshiroi:interestin,fun
onegai shimasu:Please (I
    request)
onsen:hot spring
orimasu:orite:oriru:
    to get down
osake:sake:rice wine
oshiemasu:oshiete:oshieru
    to teach
oshiro:castle
osoi:late, slow
otearai:restroom
otera:temple
oai shimashō:Let's meet
okaeri nasai:welcome
            home

P:
pen:pen
pēji:page
posto:mailbox

R:
raishū:next week
resutoran:restaurant
ryokan:inn
ryokō:trip

S:
sakana:fish
sake:rice wine
samui:cold
san:3
san:Mr. Mrs. Miss
sayonara:good bye
seito:student,puple
sensei:teacher
shashin:picture,photo
shatsu:shirts
shi:4
shichi:7
shima:island
shimaimasu:shimatte:shimau:
    to put away
shimasu:shite:suru:to do
shimemasu:shimete:shimeru:
    to close
shinbun:newspaper
shinkansen:new bullet train
shinsetsu:kind
shiro:castle
shiroi:white
shizuka:quiet
shokuji:meal
shukudai:homework
sō:so
soko:there, that place

sono: that+(noun)
sore: that thing
sorekara: and then
soto: outside
suki: pleasing, to like
sumimasu: sunde: sumu:
    to live
sushiya: sushi shop

T:
tabemasu: tabete: taberu:
    to eat
tachimasu: tatte: tatsu:
    to stand up
tai desu: to want to..
taitei: most of the case
takai: expensive
takushii: taxi
tanoshii: enjoyable
tegami: letter
tenpura: tenpura, deep
    fry
ten-in: store clerk
tera: temple
terebi: T.V.
to: door
tōi: far
toire: toilet
tokei: watch, clock
tokidoki: sometimes
tokoro: place
tomarimasu: tomatte: tomaru
    to stop, stay overnight
tomodachi: friend
torimasu: totte: toru:
    to take, to pick up
tsukaremasu: tsukarete:
    tsukareru: to be tired
tsukimasu: tsuite: tsuku:
    to arrive
tsukurimasu: tsukutte:
    tsukuru: to make
tsumaranai: dull
tsumetai: cold(thing)

U:
umi: sea
untenshu: driver

W:
wa: as for..
wakarimasu: wakatte: wakaru:
    to know, understand
warui: bad

Y:
yama: mountain
yasai: vegetable
yasashii: easy
yasui: cheep
yōhuku: western clothes
yomimasu: yonde: yomu:
    to read
yoroshiku: remember me
yon: 4
yūbinkyoku: post office
yuka: floor
yūmei: famous
yukkuri: slowly

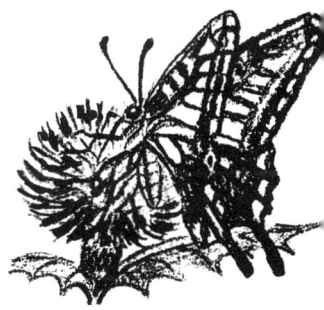

Appendix 14: Additional Vocabulary: Food

たべもの	tabemono	food
のみもの	nomimono	drink
みず	mizu	water
おちゃ	ocha	tea
ごはん	gohan	cooked rice, a meal
あさごはん	asa gohan	breakfast
ひるごはん	hiru gohan	lunch
ばんごはん	ban gohan	supper
しょくじ	shokuji	a meal
おにぎり	onigiri	rice ball
おすし	osushi	sushi
うどん	udon	noodle
おかし	okashi	sweet, cake
おやつ	oyatsu	snack
せんべい	senbei	cookie
あめ	ame	candy
さかな	sakana	fish
えび	ebi	shrimp
てんぷら	tenpura	deep fried
さしみ	sashimi	raw fish dish
にく	niku	meat
やきとり	yakitori	barbecued chicken
てりやき	teriyaki	barbecued meat
すきやき	sukiyaki	beef dish
やさい	yasaki	vegetable
にんじん	ninjin	carrot
ねぎ	negi	onion
ほうれんそう	hōrensō	spinach
つけもの	tsukemono	pickles
くだもの	kudamono	fruit
りんご	ringo	apple
いちご	ichigo	strawberry
ぶどう	budō	grapes
みかん	mikan	orange
もも	momo	peach
なし	nashi	pear
すいか	suika	watermelon
たまご	tamago	egg

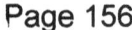

Appendix 15: Additional Vocabulary: People

ひと	hito	person, people
かぞく	kazoku	family
わたし	watashi	I, me
おや	oya	parent
りょうしん	ryōshin	parents
おとうさん	otōsan	father
おかあさん	okāsan	mother
きょうだい	kyōdai	sibling
にいさん	nīsan	elder brother
ねえさん	nēsan	elder sister
おとうと	otōto	younger brother
いもうと	imōto	younger sister
あかちゃん	akachan	baby
こども	kodomo	child
おとな	otona	adult
むすこ	musuko	son
むすめ	musume	daughter
しゅじん	shujin	husband
おくさん	okusan	wife
ふうふ	hūhu	married couple
わかもの	wakamono	young person
としより	toshiyori	old person
おじいさん	ojiisan	grandfather
おばあさん	obāsan	grandmother
おじさん	ojisan	uncle
おばさん	obasan	aunt
しんせき	shinseki	relative
おとこ	otoko	male
おんな	onna	female
せんせい	sensei	teacher
がくせい	gakusei	student
ともだち	tomodachi	friend
いしゃ	isha	doctor
かんごふ	kangohu	nurse
かいしゃいん	kaishain	company worker
てんいん	ten-in	store clerk
うんてんしゅ	untenshu	driver
じむいん	jimuin	office worker

Appendix 16: Additional Vocabulary: Places

ところ	tokoro	place
いえ	ie	house
うち	uchi	home
りょかん	ryokan	inn
おてら	otera	temple
おしろ	oshiro	castle
びょういん	byōin	hospital
しょくどう	shokudō	dining room, restaurant
きっさてん	kissaten	coffee shop
しょうがっこう	shōgakkō	elementary school
ちゅうがっこう	chūgakkō	junior high school
こうこう	kōkō	senior high school
だいがく	daigaku	college
まち	machi	town
みせ	mise	store
ちゅうしゃじょう	chūshajō	parking lot
やま	yama	mountain
もり	mori	forest
みずうみ	mizuumi	lake
おんせん	onsen	hot spring
うみ	umi	ocean, sea
かいがん	kaigan	beach
にわ	niwa	flower garden
はたけ	hatake	vegetable garden
たんぼ	tanbo	rice field
こうえん	kōen	park
のはら	nohara	field
かいしゃ	kaisha	company
ぎんこう	ginkō	bank
ゆうびんきょく	yūbinkyoku	post office
やくしょ	yakusho	government office
くうこう	kūkō	airport
えき	eki	station
バスのりば	basu noriba	bus stop
くに	kuni	nation, country
がいこく	gaikoku	foreign country
いなか	inaka	rural area, country
とかい	tokai	big town

Appendix 17: Additional Vocabulary: School

いろえんぴつ	iro enpitsu	color pencil
いろがみ	iro gami	color paper
おりがみ	origami	folding paper
かばん	kaban	book bag
ノート	nōto	notebook
はさみ	hasami	scissors
けしごむ	keshigomi	eraser
じょうぎ	jōgi	ruler
きょうしつ	kyōshitsu	classroom
でんき	denki	light
へや	heya	room
じむしょ	jimusho	office
うんどうじょう	undōjo	exercise room
おてあらい	otearai	toilet
まど	mado	window
ろうか	rōka	hall
かいだん	kaidan	stairs
いりぐち	iriguchi	entrance
と	to	door
つくえ	tsukue	desk
いす	isu	chair
せき	seki	seat
ゆか	yuka	floor
しゅくだい	shukudai	homework
べんきょう	benkyō	studying
がっか	gakka	school subject
すうがく	sūgaku	Math
りか	rika	Science
しゃかい	shakai	Social study
れきし	rekishi	History
おんがく	ongaku	Music
びじゅつ	bijutsu	Art
たいいく	taiiku	Physical Education
ひるやすみ	hiru-yasumi	lunch recess
ほうそう	hōsō	broadcasting
はた	hata	flag
こうちょうせんせい	kōchō sensei	principal
ひしょ	hisho	secretary

Appendix 18: Additional Vocabulary: Time, Day, Year

いま	ima	now			
きょう	kyō	today			
けさ	kesa	this morning			
こんばん	konban	tonight			
こんしゅう	konshū	this week			
こんげつ	kongetsu	this month			
ことし	kotoshi	this year			
あした	ashita	tomorrow			
らいしゅう	raishū	next week			
らいげつ	raigetsu	next month			
らいねん	rainen	next year	はる	haru	spring
きのう	kinō	yesterday	なつ	natsu	summer
せんしゅう	senshu	last week	あき	aki	autumn
せんげつ	sengetsu	last month	ふゆ	huyu	winter
きょねん	kyonen	last year			
まいあさ	maiasa	every morning			
まいばん	maiban	every night			
まいにち	mainichi	every day			
まいしゅう	maishū	every week			
まいげつ	maigetsu	every month			
まいとし	maitoshi	every year			
にちようび	nichiyōbi	Sunday			
げつようび	getsuyōbi	Monday			
かようび	kayōbi	Tuesday			
すいようび	suiyōbi	Wednesday			
もくようび	mokuyōbi	Thursday			
きんようび	kinyōbi	Friday			
どようび	doyōbi	Saturday			
いっしゅうかん	isshūkan	one week			
いちじかん	ichijikan	one hour			
いちにち	ichinichi	one day			
いちがつ	ichigatsu	January			
いっかげつ	ikkagetsu	one month			
いちねん	ichinen	one year			
あさ	asa	morning			
ひる	hiru	daytime, noon			
ばん	ban	evening, night			

Appendix 19: Additional Vocabulary: Location, Counter, こそあど

Locations

うえ	ue	on, above
した	shita	under
まえ	mae	front
うしろ	ushiro	behind
なか	naka	in
そと	soto	outside
みぎ	migi	right
ひだり	hidari	left
そば	soba	by, near
となり	tonari	next to
よこ	yoko	side
はし	hashi	edge
むこう	mukō	other side, beyond
かど	kado	corner
あいだ	aida	between
まんなか	man-naka	center
きた	kita	north
みなみ	minami	south
ひがし	higashi	east
にし	nishi	west

Counters

ichi mai	one flat thing	paper, sliced ham, plate
ichi dai	one large machine	car, computer, bicycle
ippon	one long thing	pen, tree, rope, finger
ippiki	one animal	cat, dog, mouse, horse
ikken	one house	house, store, building
issatsu	one bounded thing	book, magazine
ikko	one small round thing	candy, apple, stone
issoku	one pair of shoes	stocking, shoe
ippai	one container full	water, sugar, sand

こ・そ・あ・ど

kore: this thing	kono hon: this book	koko: this place
sore: that thing	sono hon: that book	soko: that place
are: a thing over there	ano hon: a book over there	asoko: over there
dore: which thing?	dono hon?: which book?	doko?: where?

Appendix 20: Additional Vocabulary: Animals

どうぶつ	dobutsu	animal
ねこ	neko	cat
いぬ	inu	dog
ねずみ	nezumi	mouse, rat
さる	saru	monkey
ぶた	buta	pig
しか	shika	deer
たぬき	tanuki	racoon
きつね	kitsune	fox
おおかみ	okami	wolf
くま	kuma	bear
ぞう	zo	elephant
うし	ushi	cow, ox
うま	uma	horse
ひつじ	hitsuji	sheep
うさぎ	usagi	rabbit
とら	tora	tiger
とり	tori	bird
ことり	kotori	small bird
にわとり	niwatori	chicken
からす	karasu	crow
わし	washi	eagle
すずめ	suzume	sparrow
つばめ	tsubame	swallow
はと	hato	pigion
つる	tsuru	crane
あひる	ahiru	duck
さかな	sakana	fish
こい	koi	carp
さけ	sake	salmon
くじら	kujira	whale
かい	kai	clam, seashell
かえる	kaeru	frog
へび	hebi	snake
わに	wani	alligator
かめ	kame	turtle
むし	muchi	insect, worm
ちょうちょ	chocho	butterfly
とんぼ	tonbo	dragonfly
あり	ari	ant
てんとうむし	tento mushi	ladybug

Appendix 21: Additional Vocabulary: Weather & Nature

てんき	tenki	weather
はれ	hare	fine weather
あめ	ame	rain
くもり	kumori	cloudy
ゆき	yuki	snow
かぜ	kaze	wind
たいふう	taihu	typhoon
つゆ	tsuyu	rainy season
そら	sora	sky
くも	kumo	cloud
にじ	niji	rainbow
かみなり	kaminari	thunder
いなずま	inazuma	lightening
たいよう・ひ	taiyo, hi	sun
くうき	kuki	air
ちきゅう	chikyu	earth
つき	tsuki	moon
ほし	hoshi	star
みず	mizu	water
うみ	umi	sea
すな	suna	sand
かいがん	kaigan	beach
かわ	kawa	river
みずうみ	mizuumi	lake
いけ	ike	pond
き	ki	tree
まつ	matsu	pine tree
はな	hana	flower
きく	kiku	crysanthemum
さくら	sakura	cherry
くさ	kusa	grass
もり	mori	forest
のはら	nohara	field
やま	yama	mountain
おか	oka	hill
いし	ishi	stone
つち	tsuchi	dirt, soil
みち	michi	street
のうじょう	nojo	farm
たんぼ	tanbo	rice field
はたけ	hatake	vegetable garden

Appendix 22: Additional Vocabulary: Colors, Body parts

Colors

みどり	midori	green
むらさき	murasaki	purple
はいいろ	hai iro	gray
ちゃいろ	cha iro	brown
だいだいいろ	daida iiro	orange
きんいろ	kin iro	golden
ぎんいろ	gin iro	silvery

Body

からだ	karada	body
かお	kao	face
め	me	eye
はな	hana	nose
くち	kuchi	mouth
あたま	atama	head
け	ke	hair
みみ	mimi	ear
ほほ	hoho	cheek
あご	ago	chin
くび	kubi	neck
かた	kata	shoulder
ひじ	hiji	elbow
うで	ude	arm
ゆび	yubi	finger
つめ	tsume	nail
て	te	hand
あし	ashi	foot, leg
おなか	onaka	stomach
せなか	senaka	back
くちびる	kuchibiru	lips
は	ha	tooth
ひざ	hiza	knee
ひふ	hihu	skin
きんにく	kinniku	muscle
むね	mune	chest
こし	koshi	waist
ほね	hone	bone
ち	chi	blood
ちょう	chō	intestine

Appendix 23: Additional Vocabulary: Clothing, Health & Sick

Clothing

ようふく・ふく	yōhuku, huku	clothing
くつ	kutsu	shoes
うわぎ	uwagi	coat, jacket
したぎ	shitagi	underwear
ぼうし	bōshi	hat, cap
せびろ	sebiro	suits (for man)
かさ	kasa	umbrella
みずぎ	mizugi	swimming suit
きもの	kimono	kimono

Health & Sick

びょうきです	byōki desu	I am sick.
げんきが ありません	genki ga arimasen	I feel weak.
やすみます	yasumimasu	I will rest.
ねたいです	netai desu.	I want to lie down.
くすりを のみます	kusuri o nomimasu.	I take medicine.
びょういんへ いきます	byōin e ikimasu.	I'll go to the hospital
みてください	mite kudasai.	Please examine me.
けんこうです	kenkō desu.	I am healthy.
かぜを ひきました	kaze o hikimashita.	I caught a cold.
おなかが いたい	onaka ga itai.	I have a stomach ache.
げりを しました	geri o shimashita.	I have diarrhoea.
せきが でます	seki ga demasu.	I have a cough.
ねつが あります	netsu ga arimasu.	I am feverish.
めまいが します	memai ga shimasu.	I feel dizzy.
さむけが します	samuke ga shimasu.	I have chills.
ねむれません	nemuremasen.	I can't sleep.
けがを しました	kega o shimashita.	I am injured.
ちが でました	chi ga demashita.	I bled.
たべすぎました	tabesugimashita.	I ate too much.
きぶんが わるい	kibun ga warui.	I feel sick.
はが いたい	ha ga itai.	I have a toothache.
べんぴ	benpi	constipation
かゆい	kayui	itchy
なおりました	naorimashita	I recovered
おいしゃさん	oishasan	doctor
かんごふさん	kangohusan	nurse
くすりや	kusuriya	pharmacy
ふじんか	hujinka	gynecologist
けつあつ	ketsuatsu	blood presure

Appendix 24: Additional Vocabulary: House

いえ	ie	house
うち	uchi	home
たてもの	tatemono	building
へや	heya	room
いま	ima	living room
きゃくしつ	kyakushitsu	guest room
べんきょうべや	benkyō beya	study room
だいどころ	daidokoro	kitchen
しんしつ	shinsitsu	bedroom
ふろば	huroba	bathing room
おふろ	ohuro	bath tub
おてあらい	otearai	toilet
せんめんじょ	senmenjo	face wash place
げんかん	genkan	entry hall
とこのま	toko no ma	alcove
にわ	niwa	garden
ガレージ	garēji	garage
かべ	kabe	wall
てんじょう	tenjō	ceiling
ゆか	yuka	floor
たたみ	tatami	straw mat
かいだん	kaidan	stairs
にかい	ni kai	2nd floor
と	to	door
いりぐち	iriguchi	entrance
まど	mado	window
ほんばこ	honbako	book shelf
たな	tana	shelf
つくえ	tsukue	desk
いす	isu	chair
ざぶとん	zabuton	seating mat
ひきだし	hikidashi	drawer
おしいれ	oshiire	closet
ふとん	huton	bedding
まくら	makura	pillow
ねまき	nemaki	pajama
たんす	tansu	chest of drawer
でんとう	dentō	light
れいぞうこ	reizōko	refrigerator

Appendix 25: Hiragana for fun

Designing Hiragana is a fun way to memorize characters. Look at the examples. Make your own and share it with your friends.

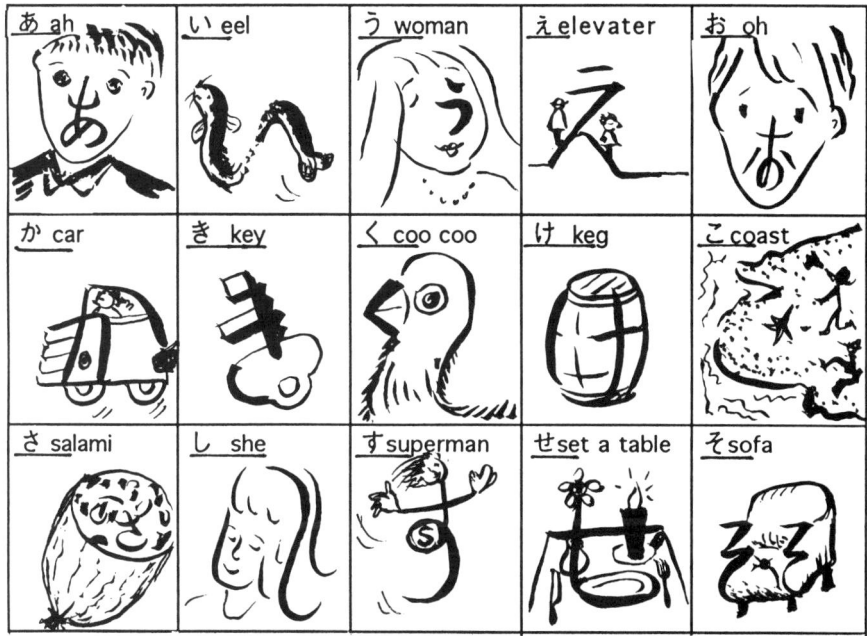

あ ah	い eel	う woman	え elevater	お oh
か car	き key	く coo coo	け keg	こ coast
さ salami	し she	す superman	せ set a table	そ sofa

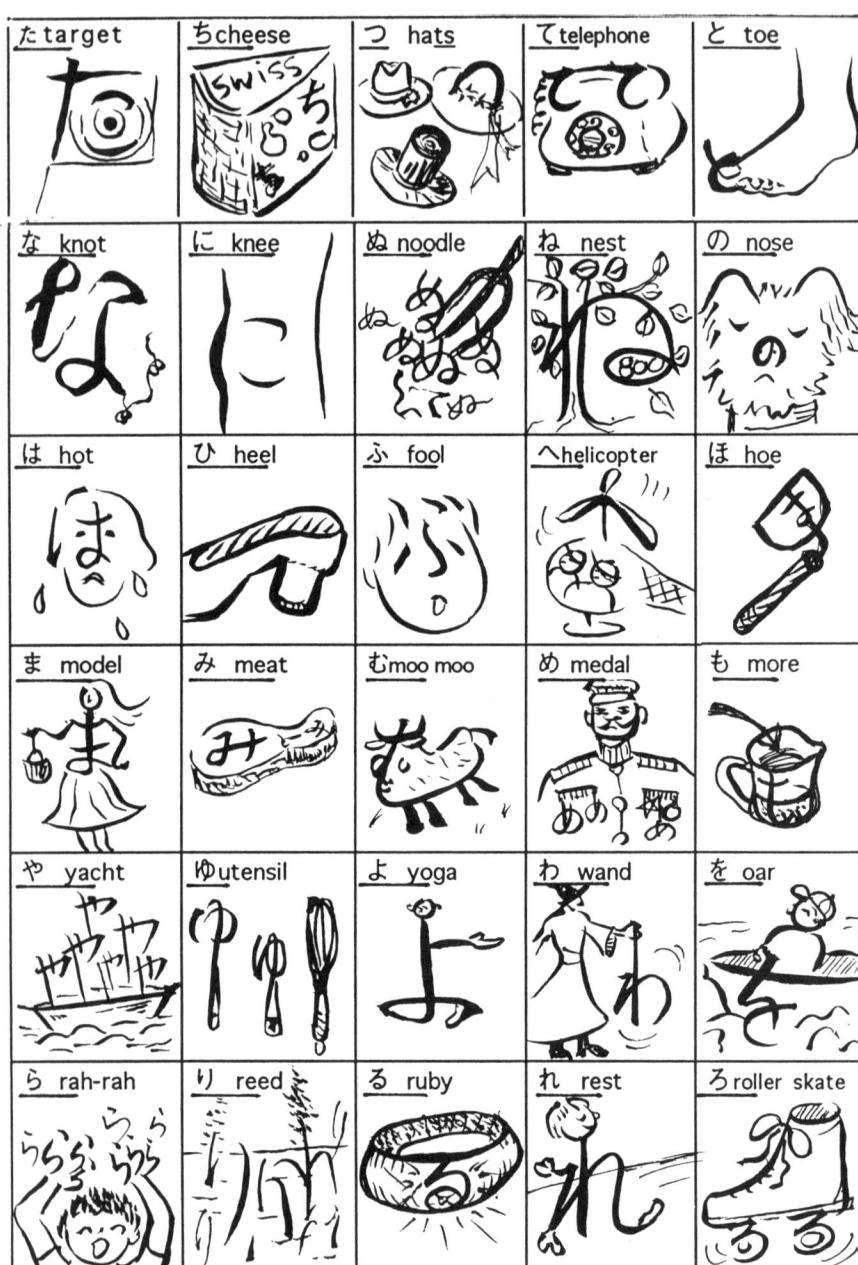

た target	ち cheese	つ hats	て telephone	と toe
な knot	に knee	ぬ noodle	ね nest	の nose
は hot	ひ heel	ふ fool	へ helicopter	ほ hoe
ま model	み meat	む moo moo	め medal	も more
や yacht	ゆ utensil	よ yoga	わ wand	を oar
ら rah-rah	り reed	る ruby	れ rest	ろ roller skate